Contemporary Issues in Mediation

Volume 10

Related Titles by the Singapore International Mediation Institute

Contemporary Issues in Mediation Volume 1
ISBN: 978-981-3108-35-6
ISBN: 978-981-3108-36-3 (pbk)

Contemporary Issues in Mediation Volume 2
ISBN: 978-981-3225-63-3

Contemporary Issues in Mediation Volume 3
ISBN: 978-981-3270-81-7

Contemporary Issues in Mediation Volume 4
ISBN: 978-981-120-911-6

Contemporary Issues in Mediation Volume 5
ISBN: 978-981-122-052-4

Contemporary Issues in Mediation Volume 6
ISBN: 978-981-124-142-0

Contemporary Issues in Mediation Volume 7
ISBN: 978-981-12-6871-7

Contemporary Issues in Mediation Volume 8
ISBN: 978-981-12-8524-0

Contemporary Issues in Mediation Volume 9
ISBN: 978-981-98-0125-1

Contemporary Issues in Mediation

Volume 10

Joel Lee
Singapore International Mediation Institute, Singapore &
National University of Singapore, Singapore
Marcus Lim
National University of Singapore, Singapore
with Felicia Leong

SIMI
SINGAPORE INTERNATIONAL MEDIATION INSTITUTE

World Scientific

Published by

World Scientific Publishing Co. Pte. Ltd.
5 Toh Tuck Link, Singapore 596224
USA office: 27 Warren Street, Suite 401-402, Hackensack, NJ 07601
UK office: 57 Shelton Street, Covent Garden, London WC2H 9HE

Library of Congress Cataloging-in-Publication Data
Names: Lee, Joel, editor. | Lim, Marcus, editor.
Title: Contemporary issues in mediation (v. 1) / Edited by Joel Lee
(Singapore International Mediation Institute, Singapore),
Marcus Lim (Singapore International Mediation Institute, Singapore).
Description: Hackensack, New Jersey : World Scientific, 2016.
Identifiers: LCCN 2016004240| ISBN 9789813108356 (hardcover : alk. paper) |
ISBN 9789813108363 (pbk.)
Subjects: LCSH: Dispute resolution (Law) | Mediation. | Dispute resolution (Law)--Singapore. |
Mediation--Singapore.
Classification: LCC K2390 .C667 2016 | DDC 347/.09--dc23
LC record available at http://lccn.loc.gov/2016004240

Contemporary issues in mediation (v. 10)
ISBN 9789819825035
ISBN 9789819825042 (eBook)
ISBN 9789819825059 (mBook)

British Library Cataloguing-in-Publication Data
A catalogue record for this book is available from the British Library.

For any available supplementary material, please visit
https://www.worldscientific.com/worldscibooks/10.1142/14639#t=suppl

Typeset by Stallion Press
Email: enquiries@stallionpress.com

https://doi.org/10.1142/9789819825042_fmatter

Endorsements

"The articles featured in this milestone tenth edition of *Contemporary Issues in Mediation* showcase the growing level of sophistication and thought leadership that has emerged over the years to impact the mediation landscape. I was drawn in particular to the articles on Individual Mediators as Peacemakers on a global stage and the article on narrative mediation. The first has a crisp analysis of the effective approaches of mediators who were involved in well- known national or cross-border conflicts. In the second, I appreciated the value of "unique route of questioning…", aimed at de-escalation and cooperation.

For those in this space, we are keenly aware of how mediation has been developing in a wide range of disputes. New ideas and tools shared by students in this series add to the skill, credibility and scholarship of practicing mediators and mediation advocates alike. Thank you, CIIM, for encouraging and keeping a spotlight on this."

Shanti Abraham
IMI and SIMI Certified Mediator
International Mediator SIMC, MIMC, AAA-ICDR

"What a cornucopia of fascinating and thought-provoking articles the 10th volume provides! Spanning the timely discussion of individual mediators in international conflicts to the persistent problem of "Settlers' Remorse", each article is well researched, beautifully written and essential reading for all mediators worldwide.

Rachael Quek's winning article on mediators as peacemakers in international conflicts is particularly relevant in today's war torn world; with Tan Yuxuan's discussion advocating a narrative approach to mediation, these are two fascinating examples of the expanding global influence of mediation.

The article describing how mediation overcomes barriers to justice addresses the problem of inequality when one disputant lacks socio-economic and financial capital. Complementing this is a fascinating comparison between the Lord Krishna's role as Shantidoot in the Mahabharata and the discussion of what neutrality means in facilitative and evaluative mediation and how far neutrality affects a mediator's conduct.

The articles on the Singapore Convention were of particular interest for me, as a member of the UNCITRAL II working party that drafted it, particularly the analyses of Articles 5 (1)(e) and (f). Finally, a fascinating discussion of anthropology as a medium for resolving disputes rounds off a rich volume of research ."

Michel Kallipetis KC
FCIArb, SIMI Certified Mediator

"At a time of great need for collaborative thinking, problem-solving, negotiation and mediation, this work emphasises the capacity of mediation to assist across a broad spectrum of disputes. Mediation is examined not only in areas of law and jurisdictions but also viz-a-vis human dilemmas. Mediators are the true peacemakers working across multiple modes of mediation as a means of access to justice.

The essence of mediation, self-determination of the parties, neutrality of the mediator and confidentiality are explored through different modes of mediation and cultural settings. Decision-making and the pivotal role of lawyers is a niche area in this volume and a timely reminder to advocates of the skills required to effectively represent their clients in ADR frameworks including mediation.

Finally, the raison d'etre for the Singapore Convention, the role of the state in investor-state mediation, and third-party funding are also examined. I commend this rich publication to all peacemakers and those involved in the administration of justice. Congratulations to SIMI on this new volume of essays."

Mary Walker OAM
Barrister, Mediator, Dispute Resolution Practitioner and SIMI Certified Mediator

https://doi.org/10.1142/9789819825042_fmatter

Contents

https://doi.org/10.1142/9789819825042_fmatter

Foreword for the Series

William Ury

A young man was hiking through the woods. He came to a clearing and sat on a rock to rest. As he ate his lunch, he noticed an old man moving through the clearing in a very deliberate way. The man would walk a specific number of steps, poke a hole in the ground with his walking stick, drop something in and then repeat the process. Curious, the young man approached the old man and asked him what he was doing.

> The old man replied, "Well, I'm planting trees."
> "But why?" the young man asked.
> "When I was younger," the old man said, "this entire land was filled with trees. But over time, many trees had been cut down.
> I come here every day to plant trees."
> Fascinated, the young man asked, "How long have you been doing this?"
> "Forty years." was the matter of fact reply.
> "Forty years!" exclaimed the young man.
> "Yup," the old man replied. Gesturing to a grove of young trees in the distance, he said with some pride, "I planted those 10 years ago."
> The young man was incredulous. "That's great but these trees will take a long time to grow! And, if you will pardon me saying so, you may not live long enough to see the seeds you are planting today grow into trees!"
> "This is true," said the old man "I have lived long enough to see some of the fruits of my labour. But the seeds I plant today are not for me, but for you."

It has now been just about 40 years since I had the privilege of embarking on the adventure of teaching and practicing in the field of negotiation and mediation. During that time, I have had the joy of learning from and working with many highly talented and skilled individuals in academia, law, business and diplomacy. In those early days, there was very little scholarly writing in this area. After all, the field was relatively new and viewed by many with caution, if not outright skepticism.

Over the years, I have been gratified to watch the field of mediation grow considerably. Today, practitioners, teachers and researchers can be found in every part of the world. The teaching, practice and scholarship of negotiation and mediation constitute a dynamic system in which each contributes to the others. New tools and frameworks have been developed as a result of research, taught to practitioners, and then tested and refined in the field, which in turn has informed further research. This interplay between theory and practice has been vital in developing new insights and methods.

Yet the field of negotiation and mediation is still young. As we look back on the progress, we might be satisfied with the seeds we have planted which have sprouted into trees. Yet, as the concepts and practices spread around the world, we have a responsibility to ensure that future generations will be able to build on all that has been achieved. We must continue to plant seeds, not for ourselves, but for those to come.

This is why this book project by the Singapore International Mediation Institute is such a timely endeavour worthy of support. It is said that a journey of a thousand miles begins with a single step. The Singapore International Mediation Institute is taking that first step to inspire the youth of today and encourage them to engage in scholarship about mediation. It provides them the platform and the opportunity to plant seeds for the benefit and enjoyment of future generations.

As the first of its kind in Singapore, I look forward to seeing this book series not only continue to flourish, but also to show the way forward through innovative and thought-provoking work.

And I take this opportunity to wish you much success in getting to yes!

William Ury
Co-founder, Harvard Negotiation Project
Co-author, *Getting to Yes*
31 May 2016

https://doi.org/10.1142/9789819825042_fmatter

About the Editors

Joel Lee is a Professor at the Faculty of Law, the National University of Singapore. Joel co-pioneered the teaching of Negotiation and Mediation in the Singapore Universities and has played a significant role in furthering the development of mediation in Singapore, not just in education but in practice. A graduate of Victoria University of Wellington and Harvard Law Schools, Joel is a principal mediator with the Singapore Mediation Centre and a Master Trainer with Peacemakers.

Joel was a member of the International Mediation Institute's Independent Standards Commission and Intercultural Taskforce and was also a key member of the Ministry of Law's Working Group on International Commercial Mediation. Joel is presently the founding Chair of the Board of the Singapore International Mediation Institute. He is also a Certified Trainer of Neuro-Linguistic Programming (NLP).

Joel has taught overseas at the University of Copenhagen (Denmark), University of Law, Economics and Science of Aix-Marseille (Aix-en-Provence France) and Anglia Law School (UK) and is the co-editor and co-author of the book *An Asian Perspective on Mediation* and the *Singapore Mediation Handbook*, and the General Editor for the *Asian Journal on Mediation*. In 2011, Joel was awarded the Outstanding Educator Award which is the National University of Singapore's highest teaching award. Joel was also awarded the Singapore's Public Service Medal in 2023 for his work in promoting mediation.

Marcus Lim is an Adjunct Associate Professor for Negotiation and Mediation Workshops at the Faculty of Law, National University of Singapore and has taught at the faculty since 2015. He is also an Associate Trainer with the Civil Service College. A graduate from the prestigious Law and Business Double Degree programme at the National University of Singapore, he is certified in the Thomas-Kilmann Instrument for Conflict and Change Management. Marcus is a SIMI Certified Mediator, an Associate Mediator with the Singapore Mediation Centre and a court-appointed volunteer mediator for the Small Claims Tribunal at the State Courts.

Marcus was the first Executive Director, and later CEO, of the Singapore International Mediation Institute (SIMI), where he spearheaded many initiatives in growing the organisation into an internationally recognised and credible brand for mediation standards. Prior to joining SIMI, Marcus practised at Rajah & Tann LLP's Competition and Technology, Media and Telecommunications Practice Group. He has held senior management roles at an international legal technology company and currently engages in training and financial consultancy.

Marcus has extensive experience conducting conflict management training for staff and management of government organisations and multinational corporations across a diverse range of sectors, such as finance, retail, real estate, IT, education and the healthcare industry.

Felicia Leong is a recent graduate of the Faculty of Law, Singapore University of Social Sciences (SUSS). She won the national round of the International Negotiation Competition (INC) and represented Singapore at the 2023 finals in Rome, Italy, placing sixth internationally. That same year, she received the National SMU–SIMI Centre for Dispute Resolution (CDR) Award, recognising her contribution to and promotion of collaborative dispute resolution in Singapore. Felicia has remained active in legal education, coaching SUSS Law's INC teams in 2024 and 2025 and designing simulation-based training that builds students' skills in case theory, interest-based negotiation, and mediator-party communication.

https://doi.org/10.1142/9789819825042_fmatter

Editors' Note

In this tenth and final volume of Contemporary Issues in Mediation ("CIIM"), we bring to a close a series that has traced mediation's journey from being a promising alternative to an essential pillar of modern dispute resolution. The essays gathered here are both outward-looking and inward-examining. The essays grapple with conflicts across borders and institutions while considering the principles, incentives and professional judgements that sustain the craft.

We begin with the human architecture of peacebuilding. By examining how individual mediators calibrate mandate, timing and leverage to context, one contribution shows how personal legitimacy can shift the trajectory of international conflicts (Quek Jia Ying Rachel). A complementary lens urges ethnography-led, identity-affirming process design such as adopting local rituals and histories, to steer between cultural imperialism and uncritical relativism across linguistic and social borders (Ng Hui En Helene). Drawing wisdom from the Mahabharata, the poem reminds us that party agency, trust and commitment are often the decisive variables; mediator virtuosity helps, but ownership by the disputants is what sustains settlement (Gauri Yadav). Together, these pieces insist that process must fit people, not the other way round.

The collection then examines technique and professional ethics. A careful unpacking of neutrality moves us beyond rigid labels (facilitative versus evaluative) to a behavioural ethic, to disclose and equalise, so that the process protects fairness while allowing context-sensitive intervention (Lee En Jia Chloe). In the same vein, a case for the narrative approach shows how counsel and mediators can responsibly harness storytelling and reconstructing, without eroding party autonomy or mediator impartiality (Tan Yuxuan). Completing this practice-facing arc, we are reminded that to prevent settlement regret, counsel must set clear expectations, equip clients to make informed choices and maintain procedural justice, otherwise, even well-constructed agreements can fray (Tay Theng Shuen). Woven through is a wider concern with access to justice: the value of mediation lies not only in speed or cost, but in voice, inclusion and the fair distribution of power at the table (Dr Emadeldien Hussein).

A third cluster tests the institutional spine of cross-border practice. A collaborative reading of the Singapore Convention on Mediation and the New York Convention reads as two pieces of a puzzle, whereby they are distinct in purpose, yet complementary when properly sequenced in tiered dispute clauses and Arb-Med-Arb pathways (Meghna Jandu). The debate on mediator standards under Article 5(1)(e) of the Singapore Convention asks when safeguards genuinely protect users and when over-specification chills innovation and party autonomy. The proposed way forward is to aim for balance — enough safeguards to ensure fairness but flexible enough for parties to share the process (Mervyn Lin Zheng Hong). A policy analysis of third-party funding cautions that extending funding to stand-alone mediation raises acute concerns, such as confidentiality, control, incentives, that current practice and public policy must resolve before broad adoption (Neo Win Kyi). Finally, in mediating investor–state disputes, confidentiality and transparency should be balanced by keeping talks discreet for candour but provide measured public visibility for accountability (Ng Xin Yu).

The earlier volumes charted possibilities and Volume 10 consolidates these lessons. Mediation thrives when it is culturally intelligent, norm-conscious and institutionally grounded; when it balances confidentiality with legitimacy; and when advocates, mediators and parties alike attend to story, explore and resolve. We hope this valedictory volume equips peacemakers, in courtrooms, boardrooms and conflict zones, to carry the work forward with nuance, courage and care.

This will be the concluding volume of CIIM, and this publication would not have been possible without the support and effort of many people. We would like to take this opportunity to express our heartfelt thanks to:

- All of CIIM contributors over the years;
- Our wonderful families, for their unending patience and love;
- Ms Felicia Leong, for her dedicated and invaluable professional assistance to the editorial team;

- Mr William Ury, for writing the foreword for the series;
- Members of SIMI's board, past and present for their unwavering support of the project (Ms Charlene Chang, Professor Nadja Alexander, Mr Poon Hong Yuen, Mr Han Kok Juan, Mr Calvin Phua, Ms Josephine Hadikusumo, the late Mr Michael Leathes and Ms Irena Vanenkova);
- The Singapore Ministry of Law, for continuing to support our work;
- The National University of Singapore Faculty of Law, for being a stalwart supporter of SIMI's operations;
- Our publishers, the World Scientific Publishing Company for their patience and guidance in bringing our final volume to publication and for their stalwart support over the years; and
- Our students (past and present) from the National University of Singapore Faculty of Law, the Singapore Management University Yong Pung How School of Law, the Singapore University of Social Sciences School of Law, as well as all over the world, who have always been an inspiration to our work.

Last but not least, we would like to thank you, the reader, for supporting SIMI and this book. We hope that this project continues to inspire you in your work, whatever field it may be, to find collaborative solutions in resolving your disputes.

Joel Lee and Marcus Lim
Editors for CIIM 10
10 September 2025

https://doi.org/10.1142/9789819825042_fmatter

About the CIIM Essay Competition

As part of SIMI's (Singapore International Mediation Institute) mission to promote awareness and interest in mediation, SIMI has for the past 10 years organised an essay competition to help promote mediation academia among undergraduates and students in tertiary institutions. Submissions came from students not only pursuing studies in law but also other disciplines. Every year, selected entries were featured in that year's edition of *Contemporary Issues in Mediation*, with attractive prizes for some of the best submissions.

About SIMI

The Singapore International Mediation Institute (SIMI) was incorporated on 15 July 2014 as a non-profit organisation supported by the Ministry of Law. SIMI is a subsidiary of the National University of Singapore (NUS) and is housed at the NUS Faculty of Law.

SIMI is headed by an international Board of Directors with representatives from both mediation practitioners as well as corporate users of mediation, to further its mission to (1) set and achieve high mediation standards through the professionalisation of mediation; (2) promote understanding and inspire the use of mediation; (3) stimulate and facilitate the development and growth of mediation through research and innovation; and (4) foster a strong mediation community in Asia by engaging stakeholders in discussion, events and outreach activities.

https://doi.org/10.1142/9789819825042_0001

Chapter 1

Peacemakers: Individuals as Mediators of International Conflicts

Quek Jia Ying Rachel

I. Introduction

In recent years, there has been a remarkable expansion in mediation efforts alongside a growing diversity of international mediators, as international conflicts get increasingly complex. This shift entails a departure from mediations predominantly led by the United Nations towards greater involvement of regional organisations, states and independent mediators such as esteemed individuals.[1]

Some have argued that individual mediators demonstrate the lowest effectiveness in reaching settlements in international disputes[2] and recent scholarship seems to discount individual mediation entirely to focus on international mediation by states, international and regional organisations, and non-governmental organisations. However, there have been success stories of individual mediation, which demonstrate how strategies adopted by individuals can allow them to fill the gaps that mediation by international institutions, regional organisations or states are unable to.

This paper provides deeper insights into the existing literature on individual mediation of international conflicts and demonstrate that individuals should not be overlooked as effective mediators for disputes between states, especially when alternative international actors fail to intervene. Through various case studies, this paper will analyse the strategies adopted by individual mediators that enabled them to overcome the challenges and deadlocks of the conflict resolution process.

II. International Mediation and the Limitations of Individual Mediators

In Touval and Zartman's[3] widely cited typology, three different approaches adopted by mediators in international conflicts are characterised. First, the mediator as a communicator focusses on facilitating improved understanding and communication between the parties. The communication-facilitation strategy falls within the low end of the intervention spectrum, with the mediator usually taking on a relatively passive stance. The mediator conveys information to the parties and fosters collaboration but exerts minimal influence over the substance or formal process[4] of the mediation.

Second, the mediator as a formulator focusses on organising aspects of the mediation process. Procedural strategies allow the mediator to exercise greater formal authority over the mediation process in relation to the environment of the mediation. It may involve roles such as determining the structural elements of meetings, managing constituency influences, handling media publicity, controlling information distribution and leveraging the situational powers of the parties' resources and communication objectives.[5]

Third, the mediator as a manipulator focusses on the objective and perceptual dimensions of the dispute's substantive content. The mediator adopts directive strategies, which involve high levels of intervention, as they influence the content and substance of the mediation by offering incentives or issuing ultimatums. These directive strategies directly address and seek to alter the framing of issues and the associated behaviours of disputing parties.[6]

Studies have shown that directive strategies, characterised by greater mediator involvement, persistence, and assertive efforts, prove more effective in achieving settlements in high-intensity disputes. Conversely, the least intrusive strategy, communications facilitation, consistently yields inferior results even though it is most frequently used by international mediators. Therefore, the degree of intervention and the effectiveness of the strategy can depend on the intensity of the dispute.[7]

High-intensity disputes refer to difficult and less amenable conflicts which attract global attention and likely involve third-party states.

In high-intensity conflicts, the effectiveness of directive strategies and international organisation mediators, such as the United Nations, stems from their abundant resources, esteemed reputation, and detachment from the dispute[8] which allows them to have higher mediator involvement and persistent, intrusive efforts which are effective when it comes to facilitating the achievement of a comprehensive settlement.

On the other hand, procedural strategies and mediation by regional organisations demonstrate effectiveness in managing low-intensity conflicts due to their familiarity with the key actors, cultural affinity, relative informality and lower costs, and the potential alignment of key actors with specific sides in the dispute enhances their efficacy in achieving outcomes.[9] In contrast, the universal composition and formal diplomatic machinery of international organisation mediators may potentially hinder rather than facilitate dispute resolution efforts in low-intensity disputes.[10]

Individual mediation, carried out by non-official or non-political incumbent individuals, is rare and typically supplements the formal pre-negotiation endeavours of conflict resolution. Due to their limited resources and the associated costs and risks required to adopt directive strategies, they were found to be the least successful in achieving settlements.[11,12] Individual mediators typically adopt communication-facilitation strategies which have shown the least effectiveness in achieving settlements in both high and low-intensity disputes. Therefore, individual mediators are the least effective in resolving international disputes.[13]

III. Martti Ahtisaari and the Aceh Peace Process

Without the appointment of Martti Ahtisaari as an individual mediator, the Aceh Peace Process between the Free Aceh Movement ("**GAM**") and Indonesia would not have started due to disagreements between parties. Indonesia viewed the conflict with GAM as an internal affair and opposed the involvement of third-party states or any formal mediator, effectively also ruling out international and regional organisations. The GAM sought independence for the Aceh region from Indonesia and wanted to internationalise the conflict through the appointment of a mediator.[14]

As a former president of Finland, Ahtisaari's connection with European states and experiences in mediating several conflicts around the world provided the peace process with the prestige and international personality that GAM leaders wanted, but also promised a fair and impartial process. The Indonesian government's concerns were quelled as Ahtisaari was retired and no longer an official or active statesman, ensuring that his mediation of the conflict would remain informal and would not officially internationalise the conflict and Aceh's status.[15]

Additionally, Ahtisaari was unafraid to apply directive strategies and encouraged the involvement of other international actors as an individual mediator. Ahtisaari actively engaged with the substantive issues of the dispute. First, Ahtisaari applied pressure on GAM to abandon its pursuit of independence, aligning with Indonesia's position that Aceh should remain part of the country. Ahtisaari departed from a position of neutrality as a mediator and leveraged the asymmetry between parties to maintain the momentum of the negotiation.[16]

To balance it out, Ahtisaari adopted flexible agenda-setting that enabled GAM to introduce the political solution of self-governance for Aceh to navigate between Indonesia's initial insistence on "special autonomy" as a precondition and GAM's insistence on full independence from Indonesia.[17] Using the open-ended term of "self-government", GAM had more autonomy during the negotiations with Indonesia to define what Aceh "self-government" would entail without being hand-tied by the already politically charged "special autonomy" term.[18] Consequently, a win-win situation emerged — an unusual success in the realm of secessionist conflict, which typically results in a win-loss dynamic.[19]

One of the reasons for this success was how Ahtisaari wielded significant influence over the agenda — by ensuring the inclusion of other important issues on the agenda and refusing to discuss issues absent from the agenda. On numerous occasions during the negotiations, Ahtisaari threatened to withdraw as the mediator when issues, such as the debate over autonomy versus full independence posed a significant obstacle for the negotiations to continue.[20] It can be seen that Ahtisaari demonstrated a considerable degree of coercive potential and vested interests in the outcome of the Aceh peace process even though he was a private, non-state and informal individual mediator.[21] Nonetheless, Ahtisaari possessed sufficient authority over the process that provided him with significant political leverage which he used to ensure the implementation of the 2005 Memorandum of Understanding ("**MOU**").

On the need for international monitors, Ahtisaari was able to secure the parties' agreement and the commitment of the European Union ("**EU**") and the Association of Southeast Asian Nations ("**ASEAN**") to monitor the MOU's implementation through the establishment of a joint EU-ASEAN Aceh Monitoring Mission ("**AMM**") with his persuasive influence.[22] Although Indonesia might have been open to some kind of regional monitoring through ASEAN, this proposition would have been unacceptable to GAM due to Indonesia's substantial regional status and influence among the ASEAN countries. This is why Ahtisaari brought in the EU, believing that EU involvement in the implementation would serve as a crucial counterweight to ASEAN monitors, provided that the participation of both organisations could be negotiated.[23]

After initial discussions concluded, Ahtisaari sought to encourage Indonesia to contemplate the possibility of including EU monitors by arguing that the EU was not itself a government despite being composed of member governments and was not classified as an international organisation. Contingent on ASEAN's involvement, the combined auspices would alleviate Indonesia's concerns.[24] Highlighting the constraints of time, finances and patience of external actors, Ahtisaari insisted that both parties express their commitment to permitting ASEAN and EU monitors to oversee the disarmament.[25] Ahtisaari's approach garnered both parties' support for a combined mission of 200 unarmed monitors to oversee the implementation of the MOU.[26]

Eight months after the start of the Aceh Peace Process, Ahtisaari ensured both a settlement through the MOU and the implementation of the MOU's provisions through the establishment of AMM, which has been widely regarded as highly successful.[27] The AMM was supported by significant institutions and wielded substantial political leverage during the crucial concluding phase of conflict resolution, which is equally sensitive and important.[28]

Although he was an individual mediator with no tangible resources other than his connections, Ahtisaari was unafraid to use directive strategies in mediating a high-intensity secessionist conflict and bolstered his leverage in the negotiation process by involving other international actors, as well as borrowing their resources and influence.[29]

IV. George Mitchell and the Good Friday Agreement

Beyond the three broad classes of mediator action characterised by Touval and Zartman,[30] actions by an individual mediator can fall into all three categories and take a form of its own. The mediation strategies adopted by George Mitchell, former United States Senate Majority Leader, who was appointed by the British and Irish governments to co-chair the All-Party Peace Talks in Northern Ireland in 1996, could give rise to another type of mediator — "mediator as a coalition-builder",[31] especially in multi-party situations.

Mitchell's involvement as mediator between the parties played a pivotal role in reaching the Belfast Agreement, signed on Good Friday in 1998, which ended the violence that had plagued Northern Ireland since the 1960s. This took place despite key barriers such as profound psychological rifts resulting in political polarisation, irreconcilable positions on substantive issues, the absence of a recognised framework and accepted process, and the absence of instruments of formal influence such as financial or military resources.[32]

Mitchell's strategy encompassed certain choices with regard to the design, timing of the process and management of the issues, all of which enabled him to overcome the obstacles and create a central coalition which ultimately propelled the process towards reaching an agreement.

First, Mitchell placed a "relentless focus" on prioritising negotiations on the process rather than substance, allowing him to gain legitimacy and parties' acceptance of his authority over the negotiations to circumvent the initial resentment from unionist parties after the British and Irish governments established ground rules and appointments without consultation.[33] By centering discussions solely on procedural matters, Mitchell averted a deadlock during negotiations on substantive issues, where polarised positions could have widened the gap between negotiators.

This approach allowed parties time to express their frustrations towards the process rather than directing them towards each other. It provided an opportunity for parties to listen to one another, foster a rudimentary working relationship and achieve a successful collaboration before confronting challenging trade-offs on substantive issues.[34] Although negotiations for ground rules lasted three months, followed by another year to establish procedures and agenda, Mitchell guided the negotiation on substantive matters to a resolution in just two weeks.[35]

Moreover, Mitchell emphasised the principles of inclusion, legitimacy and consent. Parties were required to abide by the "Mitchell Principles", which outlined fundamental "commitments to democracy, dialogue and non-violence" to participate in the talks.[36] Mitchell refrained from convening meetings unless there was unanimous consent among all parties involved in deliberating the rules and procedures of the talks. This approach enabled Mitchell to assume a management role in facilitating the negotiations, consistently obtaining parties' permission to do so,[37] thereby reinforcing Mitchell's authority, enhancing the parties' trust in him and strengthening their commitment to both Mitchell and the process.

Second, Mitchell's issue management strategy focussed on two elements. Firstly, he strategically disentangled the challenging issue of decommissioning from the negotiations by proposing that discussions on decommissioning be relocated to a separate commission. This reassured the unionists that the matter remained relevant but without hindering further negotiations on other issues.[38] Secondly, the significant issues were segmented into three strands which were subsequently amalgamated into a comprehensive package that was supported by a coalition of the centre. Extended discussions on each strand allowed parties to advocate for their issues while also grasping others' perspectives. This ultimately enabled the package to appear advantageous to all parties involved, allowing it to be presented to their respective constituencies as victories.[39]

Third, to address Mitchell's lack of formal authority, the deadline tactic was used to effectively pressure action. He first demonstrated commitment to persist in the process for as long as necessary, instead of rushing into substantive issues for a premature agreement, which allowed parties to establish a foundational cooperative relationship.[40] Next, acknowledging the potential for a prolonged stalemate and lacking resources to levy sanctions or provide incentives to enforce any resolution, Mitchell strategically utilised the credibility he had accumulated over the long negotiation process to foster the parties' adherence to the deadline as a personal obligation to him and their final chance for peace.[41] Mitchell's strategy transcended the general categories of mediator action by blending mediator approaches of different degrees of intervention in a multi-party, high-intensity dispute. He successfully navigated obstacles and forged a durable coalition between eight of the ten largest political parties in Northern Ireland and the United Kingdom, culminating in a collectively acceptable and sustainable package, despite his lack of tangible resources.

V. General Abdulsalami Abubakar and the Accra Agreement

International mediation success metrics should extend beyond broad indicators like agreements, ceasefires, or the recurrence of crises. A higher degree of validity in measuring mediator success may be achieved by evaluating outcomes based on the mediators' assigned objectives, mandate or agenda.[42]

Following prevailing approaches in statistical research on international mediation, General Abdulsalami Abubakar's intervention in the July 2004 negotiations in Monrovia, as the chief mediator of the Accra Comprehensive Peace Agreement, would be perceived as a failure as it did not yield a settlement in the form of a ceasefire or peace agreement. However, his mediation efforts did significantly contribute to the effective execution of the agreement.[43]

Abubakar, the former Nigerian president, was collectively selected to be the chief mediator for peace talks between warring parties of the Second Liberian Civil War by the Economic Community of West African States and Charles Taylor, President of Liberia.[44] The Accra Comprehensive Peace Agreement, which ended the civil war in 2003, faced implementation difficulties as it stipulated a transitional power-sharing government, constitutional and electoral reforms. From 2004 to 2006, Abubakar was involved in negotiations to assist in the review of the agreement, interpretation of key provisions, and confirming signatories' commitment.[45] Abubakar's aim and responsibility was to ensure that the Accra Agreement was successfully implemented, a goal achieved through his mediation efforts, even if it did not necessarily lead to a settlement.

The determination of whether the mediation outcome is viewed as a success or failure should depend less on whether a settlement was reached, and whether the objectives outlined in the mediator's mandate were achieved by the outcome.[46] Evaluation of the effectiveness of individual mediators should move away from their sole ability to achieve settlements in international conflicts and the dichotomy between successful settlement and failure to include consideration of the agenda of the mediation and the individual mediator's given mandate.

Furthermore, while the three broad classes of mediator action may be appropriate to achieve settlement in various conflict settings, utilising them in negotiations geared towards implementing previously established settlements may prove ineffective as it may detract from problem-solving efforts.[47] For example, negotiations aimed at implementing agreements arguably require a greater emphasis on problem-solving rather than pressure from third parties, which is the signature of the directive strategy.

In this regard, during the July 2004 negotiations, Abubakar's assistance in interpreting contentious provisions of the Accra Agreement prompted the parties to reaffirm their commitment to the peace process. While his actions were on the higher end of the intervention spectrum with a focus on the substantive elements of the agreement and its implementation, he did not adopt a directive strategy. Employing incentives and threats may not have yielded a similarly positive outcome and could have divergent effects.[48]

VI. Conclusion

Examining the strategies of individual mediators such as Martti Ahtisaari, George Mitchell, and Abdulsalami Abubakar reveals the multi-faceted nature of individual mediation in international conflicts, which prevailing scholarship tends to overlook. While individual mediators may face limitations in terms of resources and formal authority, their ability to adapt to unique conflict dynamics and employ a variety of mediation strategies can prove instrumental in achieving successful outcomes. Furthermore, evaluating mediator success based on objectives outlined in their mandate rather than solely on settlement outcomes provides a more nuanced understanding of their effectiveness.

In conclusion, individual mediators play a crucial role in international conflict resolution. Mediation is an interpersonal endeavour; even when representing a state or organisation, the success of the mediation often boils down to the individuals sitting around the table. By acknowledging and understanding the strategies employed by individual mediators, policymakers and practitioners can better leverage their potential in achieving lasting peace and reconciliation in conflict-affected regions because they are more than just mediators; they are peacemakers, and the world needs them now more than ever.

https://doi.org/10.1142/9789819825042_0002

Chapter 2

Advocating for the Narrative Approach to Mediation

Tan Yuxuan

I. Introduction

Following the development of narrative family therapy by Michael White and David Epston in the 1980s,[1] the narrative model of mediation was pioneered by John Winslade ("**Winslade**") and Gerald Monk ("**Monk**"). While narrative family therapy has since risen in popularity and use, narrative mediation remains a relatively new and unexplored phenomenon in the field of mediation.[2] The theorised application of the model highlights a tension between narrative orientation and the principles of mediator neutrality and party autonomy.[3]

Although these principles are not without their flaws, it is hard to argue for an outright disregard for these concepts which have long been considered the bedrock of mediation. However, it can be observed that so far, the exploration of the narrative model has been limited to the adoption by the mediator. Conversely, much remains unexplored about how mediation advocates can use narrative strategies. Hence, this paper analyses the narrative model of mediation, its benefits and shortcomings, and explores its potential adoption by advocates. The aim is to retain the advantages of the narrative approach while avoiding its principal criticisms.

II. The Narrative Model of Mediation

A. *The Process of Mediation "from story to settlement"*

According to Winslade and Monk, people rely on narratives to make sense of their lives.[4] These stories are shaped by various dimensions of the storyteller's culture and identity. Therefore, conflict narratives arise when those facets diverge. Serving as implicit "theories of responsibility", such conflict narratives typically position the storyteller as the victim-protagonist while casting the other party as the antagonist or victimiser.[5,6]

Winslade and Monk illustrated their approach through the story of Fiona and Greg, a couple mediating a divorce after 14 years of marriage. From the outset, their positions were polarised — Fiona initiated the mediation process while Greg participated reluctantly. Fiona attributed the breakdown of their relationship to Greg's behaviour in social settings while Greg pointed to Fiona's infidelity and deception over the last three years of their marriage. Each party advanced a well-developed, problem-saturated narrative that directly competed with the other. This illustration depicts conflict at its most entrenched, where both parties cling to fixed, unyielding narratives, and regard their accounts to be the *only* true version of events.[7]

In a facilitative mediation, the mediator focusses on the settlement objective rather than the relationship aspect. The goal is not to mend the relationship or stop the divorce but rather to utilise interest-gathering techniques to surface common ground and direct that towards a solution. However, the consequence is that any agreement reached may still fall short of the ideal. In the worst-case scenario, the failure to destabilise the conflict narratives may result in an impasse with neither party willing to budge, thus ending up in the 30 per cent that fail to reach a settlement.

In contrast, the narrative model of mediation uses questioning techniques to destabilise Fiona and Greg's individual "theory of responsibility". Through a series of unique questions, the mediators create space within the closed interpretations of Fiona and Greg's conflict narratives to build an environment where both become more willing to collaborate before turning to the dispute itself.

To loosen such tightly woven stories, the mediator must first build rapport with the parties, as narrative probing may come off as biased against one party's story. Hence, a well-trained mediator is able to rework aspects of an emotionally-ridden story and convey understanding without reinforcing these problem-saturated descriptions.

Winslade and Monk highlight externalising conversations as one of the most powerful methods that narrative practitioners can use. Through the identification of common themes such as emotions, the mediator can isolate these themes and discuss them as if they were external forces, and not inherent flaws in either party. Bringing what parties have so deeply internalised to the surface allows everyone to examine it from a neutral lens. After this, the mediator "maps" the conflict timeline, using direct questions to flesh out the conflict history.

A valuable line of inquiry for the mediator is to invite the parties to consider the effects of the conflict. In the case of Fiona and Greg, the mediator asked them to consider the effect of prolonging the marital and custody dispute on their three children. Confronted with this perspective, Greg, who had been reluctant to consider how the conflict had been affecting his children, wavered from his adversarial stance to reconsider prolonging the custody dispute because he did not want to cause more distress for his children.

A unique route of questioning involves constructing new narratives. Instead of the usual "chunking up or down" questions which is taught in traditional interest-gathering, the mediator may pose questions that seem unrelated to the dispute itself. Focussed on de-escalation, the mediator asked Greg to recall positive interactions with Fiona, where trust was built rather than lost. This tactic prevents negative experiences from monopolising the couple's history and simultaneously, co-authors a new narrative that reframes their relationship. The result is a more cooperative atmosphere for resolving the present dispute and to build a better platform for future conflicts to be settled.

It should be noted that conflicting parties in reality may not be as contentious as Fiona and Greg were. Winslade and Monk chose an extreme case of conflict to demonstrate the narrative model's ability to destabilise conflicts, but focussing too much on this case can overemphasise the necessity of destabilising as a precursor to settlement. Depending on the case, it is possible to reach a fair settlement without having to break down the conflict narratives, but the benefits of the narrative approach in bettering the relationships and easing conflicts are universal. There is value in further observation of the narrative model in its theoretical form, comparing it against the "traditional" problem-solving framework.

B. *The Three Phases of Narrative Mediation*

In the wake of postmodernism,[8] the narrative model embraces each parties' interpretation of the conflict narrative rather than seeking an objective "truth". It prioritises the relational needs of conflicting parties rather than the substantive issues emphasised by the problem-solving orientation.[9]

The narrative model goes beyond simply resolving conflicts, it aims to improve communication between conflicting parties and to develop a foundation for tackling future problems.[10] To that end, the narrative-oriented mediator must work through three interconnected phases: (1) engaging the conflicting parties; (2) deconstructing and externalising primary narratives; and (3) constructing a new secondary narrative.[11]

1. **The Engagement Phase** — Alongside the usual rapport-building strategies to establish a relationship with conflicting parties, a narrative-oriented mediator must pay special attention to the non-verbal cues and identity markers, such as gender, ethnicity and culture, which may impact the conflict narratives of the parties.[12] This serves the dual purpose of strengthening the relationship between the parties and alerts the mediator to identify areas that could otherwise lead to unjust outcomes.
2. **The Deconstruction & Externalisation Phase** — This phase involves "undermin[ing] the certainties on which the conflict feeds and invite[ing] the participants to view the plot of the dispute from a different vantage point".[13] The parties will try to objectify the problem, treating it as if they were a third entity in the relationship.[14] This stage is where narrative mediation practices drastically diverge from the other models of mediation. Through this externalisation process, the mediator aims to destabilise the parties' "totalising descriptions" and to work with the parties in "co-authoring" a new and united narrative.[15]
3. **The Construction Phase** — Finally, to construct a new narrative, the mediator emphasises non-conflict interactions between the parties that employs discursive repositioning to build up a sense of hope, i.e., the conscious shaping of the discourse out of which needs and interests are produced. In doing so, this new perspective encourages parties.[16]

This has been said to improve the quality of the mediated outcomes. In contrast to the individualistic problem-solving orientation, the narrative-oriented mediators' approach seeks the underlying causes which influence the conflict narratives, making it particularly effective when working with marginalised groups.

Furthermore, research suggests that greater degrees of participation in decision-making processes and fuller opportunities to communicate their views, contribute to party satisfaction and compliance with mediated agreements.[17] Consequently, narrative mediation produces a hybrid result, it achieves the traditional settlement outcomes arising from the traditional problem-solving approach, and the empowerment, recognition, and social justice resolutions obtained from the modern transformation approach.[18]

C. *Intervention of the Mediator: Why the Narrative Model has not been widely adopted.*

Notwithstanding the aforementioned benefits, the hesitation in adopting the narrative model can be attributed to the way it is perceived to compromise the two principles of mediator neutrality and party autonomy, core concepts which many regard as being foundational in the mediation process.[19]

According to the National Mediator Accreditation System ("**NMAS**"), a mediator is expected to demonstrate an ethical understanding of neutrality and impartiality and the mediation process aims to maximise the self-determination of the participants.[20] In Singapore, the Singapore International Dispute Resolution Academy expresses the same priorities, to hold mediator impartiality and party self-determination as two of the three core values of mediation (see image below).[21]

These central concepts arise from the first generation of mediation practice[22] where problem-solving models, such as the facilitative model, evaluative model and settlement model, dominated the mediation field.[23] Unlike the narrative model, problem-solving models distinctly separate process and content[24] which is difficult or even impossible to achieve in practice, and fails to prevent unsatisfactory settlement outcomes in cases of substantive inequity.[25]

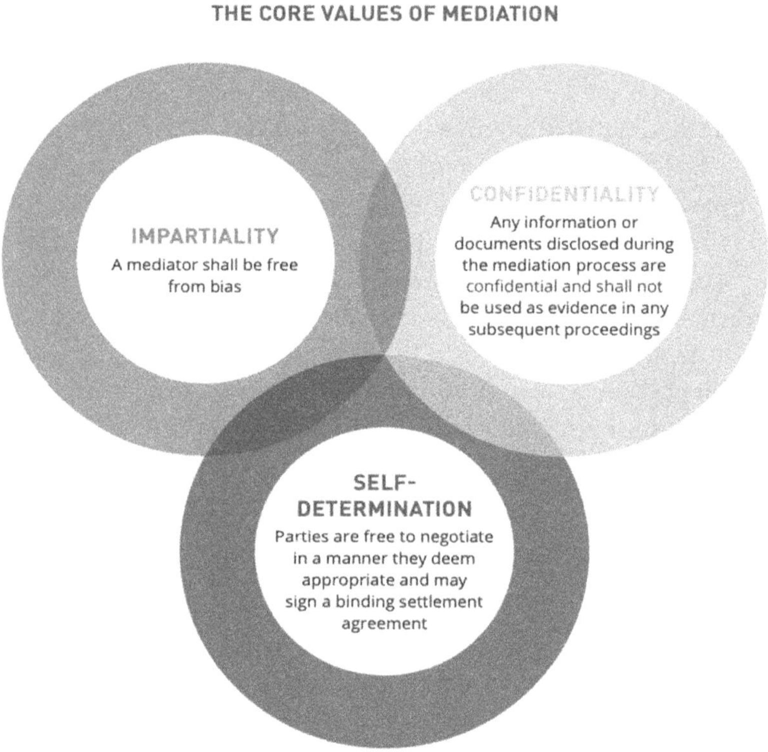

Consider a power-imbalanced dispute, where a mediator committed to neutrality is ethically barred from directly advocating for the weaker party, yet is ethically obligated to facilitate the process which instead clarifies the parties' primary discursive positions.[26] Likewise, a mediator committed to maintaining party self-determination, would allow substantively unfair settlements rather than impact the content of the dispute.[27,28]

In contrast, the narrative model does not separate process and content since it presupposes that "relationship, process, and content issues are all interwoven in the very fabric of mediation". Unlike facilitative mediators, narrative mediators are not neutral. They take an explicit position on issues of power and privilege and actively engage in reshaping the reality of experience for the parties.[29]

This model prioritises social justice and personal agency, resulting in practices which effectively promote one group of people over the other, although the extent of such promotion is yet to be definitively determined.[30] Within these secondary transformed conflict narratives, which are the mediator's "favoured versions of reality", parties can reach a solution that is socially acceptable or satisfactory compared to individual self-determination — even if substantive justice is promoted at the expense of neutrality and self-determination.

While scholars like Isabelle Gunning argue for the rejection of these two bedrock notions of mediation in favour of an approach which can uphold substantive justice,[31] the fact that these concepts have been long been entrenched in mediation "mythology" and remain touchstones for most mediator training programmes, are compelling reasons to retain or not entirely disregard these concepts.[32]

An alternative perspective could confine mediator neutrality to be limited to procedural fairness but not to the substance of the settlement agreement.[33] Jonathan M. Hyman and Lela P. Love believe that the primary role of a mediator is to facilitate justice by ensuring a fair outcome.[34] Accordingly, they contend that the mediator should ensure that an objectively fair settlement occurs in a way that would likely mirror a court-ordered result had the dispute been litigated.[35,36]

In the same vein, other scholars contend that mediators have an ethical duty and moral obligation to prevent the parties from reaching an unfair settlement agreement, regardless of the implications that may have upon the requirements of mediator neutrality and party autonomy.[37,38] No one view has been universally agreed upon, and the debate over a mediator's proper remit remains unsettled.

In any case, it is possible that we may not need to engage in this discourse at all. If we are able to succeed in having narrative-oriented mediation advocates rather than mediators, advocates could pursue socially just outcomes while the mediator continues to perform their facilitative and procedurally neutral role.

III. Towards Narrative-Oriented Mediation Advocacy

The term "mediation advocacy" can be seen as oxymoronic given the vast differences in the skills required compared to the traditional notions of trial advocacy.[39] In his article *"Mediation Advocacy: Partnering with the*

Mediator", James Lawrence ("**Lawrence**") addresses the relationship between mediator and advocate, exploring how advocates can work with mediators to achieve the best results in mediation.[40] Building on his observations, I will theorise the potential of adopting a narrative orientation to further ensure satisfactory outcomes for mediation. Thereafter, I will recontextualise the mediator's role and function once advocates adopt that perspective.

Before a mediation session, Lawrence emphasises the importance of (1) preparing the client for mediation and (2) establishing credibility with the mediator.[41] To adequately prepare the client, it is important to get the client to adopt an "open" mindset. Similar to how adversarial-litigation-based tendencies are not ideal in mediation, advocates must attempt to deconstruct positional or competitive client mindsets. Here, the advocate can refer to lines of questioning used in the Deconstruction and Externalisation phase of the narrative model (examples of the questions can be found in Annex 1) to loosen conflict stories even before the parties meet.

Meanwhile, credibility can be built through thoughtful pre-mediation submissions. Beyond stating facts and positions, Lawrence suggests that a collaborative rapport can be built through creative settlement options and by sharing the client's unique characteristics, sensitivities and emotional needs, helpful context to give the mediator a holistic picture of the barriers to settlement.[42] The narrative model can guide the advocate to better identify these characteristics and convey them to the mediator.

Ideally, both parties' advocates enter mediation with a narrative-oriented mindset. In theory, this would mean that both sides have already deconstructed the conflict stories prior to the mediation and parties are now entering the session with an open mind to collaborate and reach a settlement. The mediator's job then becomes simple, after all, "good negotiators mediate their own disputes".[43]

In such cases, there is little difference whether the mediator follows the narrative approach or one of the problem-solving models. Assuming that the advocates are well-trained in the narrative approach and in mediation advocacy in general, the outcome should be one that naturally accounts for the substantive injustice that would have otherwise been overlooked in the mediation process. The advocates trained in this approach are naturally more conscious of their client's point of view and have a deep awareness of the interests such that they can adequately protect them.

Complications may arise if one party is narrative-oriented while the other party heads into the session with a "closed" interpretation of their narrative. In this situation, there are two possible outcomes. First, if the mediator is facilitative, the mediation session will likely follow the problem-solving model progression and reach a settlement based on the primary narratives. Here, by "opening" your client's narrative at the start, it creates a risk of the client conceding to an unfavourable settlement which the advocate now needs to guard against. Alternatively, if the mediator is also following the narrative model, they can steer the discussion and deconstruct the other party's narrative during the session itself. The practical concern here would be that more time would be demanded than the parties anticipated.

Practically, the narrative model functions best when both advocates practise it. The largest barrier to the implementation would be training, since specialised training is required given that the model is not particularly intuitive.[44] Moreover, there are severe consequences should this be misapplied, such as sowing distrust between parties or parties perceiving the mediator to be biased. Nonetheless, the merits of the narrative approach cannot be overlooked and warrant pilot projects and rigorous assessments in live disputes.

IV. Conclusion

As demonstrated, there are countless benefits in adopting a narrative approach to mediation, especially in disputes regarding pre-existing social inequity, where an individual has unique characteristics which results in an imbalance of power with the opposing party. Perhaps given the practical difficulties in training persons to use the narrative method, a more workable solution is to develop a cadre of narrative-mediation specialists. These specialists could then be assigned to cases where the application of the problem-solving approach is likely to result in substantive injustice.

Appendix 1

Questions to Elicit Unique Outcomes[45]

Unique outcome questions

1. How is it that conflict did not completely stop you from wanting to talk together and find your way through the present difficulties?
2. Why did hurt feelings and blame not stop you from cancelling this meeting?
3. Do any recent occasions stand out for you in which hurt feelings and blame did not completely destroy your efforts in searching for a solution?
4. Have there been any instances recently when you experienced a hint of not being defeated by hurt feelings and blame?

Unique account questions

1. How do you explain that you were able to be more in charge of blame, humiliation, hurt feelings, or injustice than you initially thought?
2. When other people may have held on to hate, how did you develop the resources not to be dominated by blame and claim a sense of space for yourself?
3. What do you think that it means that you are agreeing about that issue?
4. How significant is it that she is willing to cooperate on your request in this case?

Unique redecoration questions

1. What does this tell you about yourself that you otherwise would not have known?
2. What does your movement away from conflict say about your ability to resolve painful difficulties?
3. Does cooperation suit you better than arguing, or not?
4. If most of the time you were able to talk civilly and respectfully about things, as you have been doing today, what would your relationship be like?

Unique possibility questions

1. Given your present understandings and your desire to heal the wounding effects of blame, what might be your next step?
2. If you were to advance the cause of cooperation, what might you try to do in the next week?
3. Now you have noticed these chances to explore greater respect in your relationship, what differences could they make?

Unique circulation questions

1. If your children were witness to these discussions, who would be most excited about this change in direction?
2. What difference would introducing more cooperation into this situation, as you have been proposing, make to your other staff or to the service you provide to your customers?
3. Who will be most likely to support the continuation of these developments?

https://doi.org/10.1142/9789819825042_0003

Chapter 3

Beyond the Classroom: Mediation and the Pursuit of Justice

Dr Emadeldien Mohamed Mahmoud Hussein

I. Introduction

Ensuring that the law remains accessible to all continues to be one of the greatest challenges of our time.[1] The fundamental objectives of the concept of "access to justice" are twofold. Firstly, it involves ensuring equitable availability of the legal system to all individuals, and secondly, the expectation that recourse in this system will ultimately result in a more just outcome.[2] This concept has been linked to the ideals of democracy and fairness and is considered a crucial aspect of the rule of law. Today, access to justice encompasses the availability of court systems, affordable legal representation, adherence to the rule of law and due process, and a system designed to provide these resources equitably to all those seeking justice.[3]

However, the expansion of transnational trade has precipitated a corresponding increase in the complexity and expense associated with litigating disputes arising from such activities. Consequently, there has been a growing recognition of the necessity for consensual methods of dispute resolution as a more efficient and cost-effective means of resolving these conflicts.[4] The emergence of increasingly complex disputes demanding specialised expertise has contributed to the growing prominence of Alternative Dispute Resolution ("**ADR**").[5]

This development coincides with the period during which scholars were actively examining the challenges associated with the concept of access to justice.[6] As a result, there is a significant overlap between ADR and the principles of access to justice. This raises the question of the link between access to justice and ADR. Essentially, access to justice refers to the "ability of individuals to seek and obtain remedies for grievances through both formal and informal justice mechanisms, in accordance with human rights standards".[7] In this context, access to justice involves the creation of dispute resolution systems, whether through traditional court processes or by utilising ADR mechanisms, with the goal of achieving swift and equitable outcomes.[8]

This essay posits that due to their ability to overcome the barriers to access to justice, ADR processes, especially mediation, have already improved and can further enhance access to justice. The essay is structured into six sections. Section I introduces the topic. Section II explores the relationship between ADR and access to justice. Section III identifies the barriers to access to justice. Section IV explains how ADR, specifically mediation, can overcome these barriers. Section V briefly proposes measures to further enhance access to justice through mediation. Finally, the conclusion summarises the findings.

II. ADR and Access to Justice

The relationship between ADR and access to justice is complex and multifaceted.[9] ADR encompasses various peaceful dispute resolution methods such as arbitration, mediation, negotiation and conciliation, as defined in Article 33(1) of the United Nations Charter. The connection between access to justice and ADR was initially recognised by Cappelletti and Garth in the late 1970s.

Initially, the traditional understanding of access to justice primarily referred to the availability of state-administered judicial systems. However, contemporary perspectives encompass the broader concept of providing individuals with effective and efficient means to resolve disputes.[10] Given the often-inaccessible nature of formal judicial systems in many parts of the world, ADR emerges as a complementary mechanism. As a result, various jurisdictions have adopted ADR as a means to facilitate access to justice, though the extent of endorsement of ADR's legitimacy may vary.[11]

This essay argues that the primary connection between ADR and access to justice lies in ADR's capacity to circumvent obstacles that discourage individuals from seeking legal remedies. To illustrate this claim, mediation will be employed as a case study to highlight its effectiveness in addressing barriers to access to justice. Defined as a process in which a disinterested or neutral third party assists disputants in reaching a voluntary settlement of their differences through an agreement that defines their future behaviour,[12] mediation aligns closely with principles of access to justice.

Unlike adversarial court proceedings, mediation operates within a flexible and informal framework, unconstrained by rigid procedural rules. This adaptability allows mediation to be tailored to the unique needs and circumstances of the parties involved.[13] Furthermore, by diverting certain disputes from overloaded courts to individual mediators, mediation can increase the overall efficiency of the legal system.[14] Unlike judicial processes, which rely on authoritative decision-making, mediation emphasises party autonomy and self-determination.[15]

III. Barriers to Access to Justice

Mauro Cappelletti ("**Cappelletti**") and Bryant G. Garth ("**Garth**"), who are considered pioneers of access to justice scholarship,[16] elucidated three primary barriers to equitable access to justice: financial burdens, relative party capability and diffuseness of interests. The financial burden imposed by court litigation constitutes the first barrier to accessing justice. Regardless of whether legal systems mandate reimbursement of the prevailing party's legal fees by the unsuccessful litigant, the process of seeking judicial remedies are frequently associated with substantial expenditure. This challenge is particularly acute in cases involving relatively minor claims, where the potential recovery may not even be sufficient to offset the cost of litigation.[17] Moreover, the delays inherent in the judicial process exacerbate these legal expenses.

Cappelletti and Garth delineate a second barrier to access to justice, which they term "relative party capability", which refers to strategic advantages enjoyed by certain litigants over others. Such advantages may manifest in the form of superior financial resources, enhanced legal acumen associated with educational attainment and socio-economic status, or extensive experience navigating the judicial system. While the correlation between financial wealth and favourable litigation outcomes is readily apparent, the impact of legal competence and repeat litigation experience is more nuanced. Individuals hailing from privileged socio-economic backgrounds often possess the requisite knowledge and skills to effectively identify and assert their legal rights. Similarly, litigants with prior experience in the legal arena may better navigate the legal intricacies of the judicial system, enabling them to exploit potential vulnerabilities.

Cappelletti and Garth identify a third barrier access to justice, "diffuseness of interests" which occurs when individuals possess fragmented and individually insignificant stakes in a dispute, rendering the financial and time-related demands of litigation disproportionate to any potential benefits. Compounding this issue, the affected individuals may be geographically dispersed, lack sufficient information regarding the matter, and struggle to coalesce around a unified strategy to address the problem.

A plethora of additional obstacles to equitable access to justice have been identified by scholars and organisations. For instance, the International Bar Association's 2014 report on international access to justice categorises these barriers into distinct domains: social, cultural, and institutional.[18] While divergent from the framework proposed by Cappelletti and Garth, these classifications exhibit substantial overlap with the aforementioned cost, relative party capability, and diffuseness of interests.

Consequently, this essay will adopt the conceptualisation advanced by Cappelletti and Garth, positing cost, relative party capability, and diffuseness of interests as the primary impediments to equitable access to justice. The subsequent section will explore the potential of mediation as a mechanism to surmount or ameliorate these challenges, thereby expanding access to justice for a broader segment of the population.

IV. How Mediation Overcomes the Barriers to Access to Justice

This section posits that mediation offers a viable strategy for overcoming or mitigating the barriers to equitable access to justice. To substantiate this position, the essay will draw upon empirical research, reports, articles, and other relevant resources to demonstrate that mediation is generally more cost-effective than traditional litigation and has the ability to balance power disparity among disputing parties.

Mediation has long been regarded as a more economically viable alternative to traditional litigation.[19] This assertion is corroborated by the surveys conducted by the Singapore International Dispute Resolution Academy in 2020 and 2022, which identified cost and efficiency as paramount factors influencing the selection of dispute resolution mechanisms.[20,21] Furthermore, the perceived cost-effectiveness of mediation is often linked to its potential to improve access to justice.[22]

For instance, a 2007 Canadian study found that mediation in selected civil law disputes improved cost and time savings by approximately 16 per cent to 17 per cent and depending on the specific characteristics of the mediation programme, this improvement could increase, potentially rising to 40 per cent.[23]

Similarly, a 2011 study within the European Union ("**EU**") to quantify the temporal and financial advantages of mediation yielded compelling results. The study focussed on Belgium and Italy, revealing significantly shorter dispute resolution timelines through mediation compared to litigation. Specifically, the study documented a 505-day litigation duration in Belgium, contrasted with a 45-day mediation process for the same type of dispute. Similarly, Italian court proceedings were estimated to take 1,210 days, while mediation could resolve the dispute within 47 days. The economic benefits of mediation were equally pronounced, with total litigation costs in Belgium and Italy amounting to 19,740 and 23,000 euros respectively, compared to mediation costs of 4,370 and 7,000 euros.

These findings strongly suggest that mediation offers considerable temporal and economic efficiency relative to litigation. A more recent empirical study conducted in 2022, examining civil and commercial mediation across Europe, reaffirmed the cost and time-saving advantages associated with mediation.[24]

However, not all research consistently supports these findings. A 2009 comparative analysis examining the economic efficiency of mediation relative to judicial review presents a divergent perspective. This particular study focussed on the realm of administrative law, assessing the utility of mediation within a public law context. A significant proportion of respondents to the 2008 study referenced in the 2009 comparative analysis posited that the costs associated with mediating public law disputes often resemble those incurred through traditional litigation.

Nonetheless, one respondent suggested that mediation might offer economic advantages in the context of commercial disputes, attributing this potential cost savings to the reduced level of preparation required for mediation compared to court proceedings.[25] Additionally, mediation has consistently faced criticism, with some arguing that its benefits, such as cost-effectiveness, are often exaggerated.[26]

While existing research presents a divergent landscape regarding the comparative cost-effectiveness of mediation and litigation, the preponderance of evidence leans towards mediation as a generally more economical dispute-resolution mechanism. The 2011 study examining mediation within the EU provides compelling evidence of substantial time and cost savings relative to traditional litigation, particularly in the context of civil disputes.[27] Conversely, the 2008 study focussing on mediation in public law disputes offers a more nuanced perspective, suggesting that while mediation may be financially advantageous in certain cases, it may not always yield significant cost reductions compared to litigation, particularly in the public law domain.[28]

Consequently, mediation's cost-effectiveness in relation to litigation is contingent upon a variety of contextual factors, including the specific nature of the dispute, the complexity of legal issues involved, and the prevailing legal framework. Nonetheless, the cumulative research strongly indicates that mediation possesses the potential to deliver substantial cost and time savings across a broad spectrum of disputes, thereby constituting a valuable instrument for enhancing access to justice.

Mediation possesses the inherent capacity to mitigate power imbalances between parties. According to Seth (2000), mediation can serve as an equaliser for marginalised and disadvantaged groups by providing a platform for their voices to be effectively heard.[29]

Further, the financial, legal, and experiential advantages identified by Cappelletti and Garth as contributing to disparities in litigant capabilities can be effectively neutralised through the strategic application of influence tactics by a skilled mediator.[30] Mediators can create equitable procedural frameworks to facilitate participation and foster a collaborative atmosphere, regardless of their individual strengths or weaknesses, thereby allowing equal opportunity to be heard and treated with respect.

Furthermore, the enhanced control and decision-making autonomy granted to parties within the mediation process significantly contrasts with the hierarchical nature of traditional litigation to further contribute to a level playing field.

However, it is imperative to acknowledge the limitations of mediation's capacity to equalise power dynamics. Instances, such as severe resource or bargaining disparities, can exacerbate vulnerabilities of the weaker party within the mediation process. In such circumstances, supplementary safeguards and proactive interventions may be necessary to prevent exploitation or coercion. Nevertheless, some scholars contend that mediation can ameliorate even the most pronounced power imbalances.[31]

Consequently, while mediation offers significant potential for empowering marginalised and disadvantaged groups, it should not be idealised as a universal panacea for addressing power disparities. A comprehensive understanding of the unique dynamics present in each dispute, coupled with judicious mediator selection and training, is essential to maximise mediation's efficacy as a tool for promoting equitable outcomes in the pursuit of justice.

The barrier to access to justice of diffuse interests identified by Cappelletti and Garth can also be addressed through the utilisation of mediation. Cappelletti and Garth's second wave of reforms sought to rectify this issue by establishing mechanisms for the representation of collective and diffuse rights. Class actions and public interest actions emerged as primary strategies for achieving this objective.[32] Mediation supports overcoming the diffuse interest barrier through its flexible procedural structure, which facilitates open communication and articulation of diverse needs and concerns among affected parties.

Greenberg and Blazina's research further underscores the potential of mediation in this domain. Their work highlights the adaptability of mediation to facilitate the resolution of class actions and mass tort claims across various litigation stages, including pre-litigation, during litigation, and post-judgement. This flexibility enables the development of tailored solutions that effectively accommodate the divergent interests of individuals impacted by a single dispute.[33]

By minimising procedural obstacles and fostering direct participation and communication, mediation empowers individuals with marginalised voices, ensuring that their interests are considered and addressed. Ultimately, mediation promotes a more inclusive and accessible approach to justice by providing a platform for the resolution of disputes involving diffuse interests.

In summary, while mediation's cost-effectiveness and ability to mitigate power disparities have been supported by numerous studies, it is important to acknowledge its limitations and the varying outcomes in different contexts. The inherent flexibility of mediation, allowing for tailored and collaborative solutions, makes it a powerful tool for enhancing access to justice, particularly for marginalised and disadvantaged groups.

To fully harness mediation's potential and address its shortcomings, deliberate measures and strategic interventions are necessary. The following section will explore these measures, examining innovative approaches and best practices that can further improve access to justice through mediation, ensuring that it remains a viable and equitable alternative to traditional litigation.

V. Measures to Improve Access to Justice Through Mediation

As we strive towards achieving a society where all individuals have equal access to justice, it is crucial to promote the responsible and effective use of mediation while acknowledging its inherent limitations. Achieving this goal requires a multi-pronged approach. Around the world, three broad trends are proving to be especially powerful.

Firstly, cost barriers are steadily eroding. A growing global recognition of mediation's efficacy is accompanied by a parallel trend towards cost reduction, facilitating broader access to this dispute resolution mechanism. In India, government-sponsored programmes offering heavily subsidised mediation sessions have emerged, while online platforms such as Mediate.com in the United States provide access to qualified mediators at reduced fees.[34] Moreover, community-led "baraza" circles in Africa offer free mediation services, promoting peace-building and lessening reliance on costly litigation.[35] These initiatives, coupled with the integration of mediation into mainstream legal services, are progressively dismantling the financial barriers to access to justice.

Secondly, mediation is used as an instrument of empowerment rather than preserving privilege. Traditionally perceived as a mechanism accessible primarily to privileged individuals, mediation is undergoing a transformative shift towards a more equitable paradigm. Contemporary initiatives are actively redefining mediation as a tool for promoting justice and empowerment. In Canada, the emergence of "trauma-informed" mediation prioritises the safety and well-being of vulnerable parties involved in domestic disputes.[36] Similarly, the development of "community-based restorative justice" circles in the United States provides marginalised groups with a platform to address conflicts according to their own values and principles, fostering healing and trust within communities.[37] These initiatives, combined with targeted training for mediators to recognise and effectively address power imbalances, are instrumental in creating a more level playing field and ensuring equitable access to justice for all.

Thirdly, the courts are increasingly encouraging the use of mediation before a case proceeds. While the efficacy of mandatory mediation remains a subject of debate, a growing trend among courts involves encouraging parties to engage in mediation as a prerequisite to formal litigation. By temporarily suspending legal proceedings to facilitate mediation, courts aim to provide litigants with a more efficient and potentially cost-effective avenue for dispute resolution. This approach has the potential to expand access to justice by offering an alternative to the often protracted and expensive legal process.

To fully realise mediation's potential as a tool for enhancing access to justice, ongoing research and evaluation are indispensable. By systematically examining mediation's efficacy across diverse contexts and assessing its impact on equitable outcomes, researchers can identify areas for improvement, refine our understanding of mediation's strengths and limitations, and develop evidence-based practices to optimise its contribution towards building a just and equitable society.

VI. Conclusion

This essay has explored the intricate relationship between mediation and access to justice, demonstrating how mediation effectively mitigates several key barriers that traditionally impede equitable access to the legal system. By offering a more cost-effective, timely, and inclusive dispute resolution mechanism, mediation is emerging as a potent instrument for empowering individuals and communities to seek justice. Recognising and promoting the responsible and effective utilisation of mediation is paramount in the pursuit of a justice system accessible to all.

While mediation offers significant advantages, it is essential to acknowledge its inherent limitations. In instances characterised by extreme power imbalances, the weaker party may remain vulnerable within the mediation process. To address this, meticulous power assessments and specialised mediator training are indispensable. Furthermore, the efficacy of mediation is context-dependent, influenced by the nature of the dispute and the mediator's expertise. Rigorous mediator selection and training are crucial for optimising mediation's potential.

Despite these caveats, the preponderance of evidence underscores mediation's capacity to substantially enhance access to justice. Its cost-efficiency, timeliness, and potential to address power imbalances position mediation as a valuable tool for individuals and communities seeking constructive dispute resolution. As society strives to achieve a more equitable and just legal landscape, the strategic integration of mediation is pivotal when trying to ensure that justice is accessible to all.

https://doi.org/10.1142/9789819825042_0004

Chapter 4

Mediating with the Mahabharata: Investigating the Parties' Influence on Success and Failure in Mediation

Gauri Yadav

I. Introduction

Conflict, whether between individuals or nations, is an inevitable part of human society. Although conflict can seem unavoidable, peace is really a choice. As Albert Einstein observed, peace cannot be kept by force; it can only be achieved through understanding. In today's world, geopolitical tensions have many countries precariously balanced between war and peace, and in this fragile climate, mediation stands as a beacon of hope. It offers a pathway that has the potential to avert the catastrophic consequences of war and holds out the hope that differences can be resolved through mutual understanding and compromise rather than violence and destruction. A successful mediation can help countries avoid armed conflict and the devastating consequences that come with that. In cases where mediation fails, history bears witness to prolonged suffering and turmoil. Whether mediation is successful will depend upon various factors, and the influence of the parties involved could be the foremost factor.

The outcome of mediation does not rest solely on the mediator's skill or neutrality. This essay explores how the actions, choices and decisions of characters acting as parties can influence conflict resolution and mediation outcomes, arguing that despite a mediator's skill and diligence, the parties' intentions, willingness to negotiate and attitudes towards the mediation process determine their courses of action and ultimately, the outcome of mediation.

To explore this dynamic, this essay draws insight from the ancient epic of India, the Mahabharata, which tells the gripping story of conflict and failed mediation that reverberates along the corridor of history to continue to have relevance in our modern world.

In the Mahabharata, mediation was attempted to resolve the difference between the Kauravas and the Pandavas (two noble families) by Lord Krishna before the outbreak of the Kurukshetra War. Despite Lord Krishna's wisdom and efforts, many factors, such as the parties' entrenched ambitions, distrust and unwillingness to compromise, ultimately shattered hopes of reconciliation and plunged Bharat (India) into the devastating Kurukshetra War. This story provides a profound understanding of how the parties involved can influence the outcome of meditation negatively, even if the mediator is competent.

By analysing various factors such as willingness, adversarial behaviour and party commitments, this essay demonstrates how these elements shaped the mediation outcomes in the epic. These insights can shed light on how the parties' influence can determine the success or failure of mediation, underscoring how similar dynamics shape modern mediation efforts. To enhance clarity, a series of tables provide an overview of the role of a mediator, the parties involved, and their relationship with other prominent characters mentioned in the essay.

II. The Significance of Parties Involved in the Mediation

Mediation is a process wherein the parties meet with a mutually selected impartial and neutral person who assists them in negotiating their differences.[1] While mediation brings together two essential actors, the parties, and the neutral mediator who facilitates the negotiation, it is ultimately the parties who hold the key to its outcome. The mediator serves as a guide, akin to a lighthouse that shines a light showing a path forward, but it is the parties who control the direction in which they move, and their ultimate destination. Alternatively, the parties can be likened to the anchors of a ship trapped in a storm, while the mediator strives to guide that ship to calmer waters. To emphasise, the mediator's role is to help parties solve the issue and avoid confrontation or ill will, but the decision-making power rests entirely with the parties.

The attitudes and actions of the parties involved profoundly influence the outcome of the mediation. The parties' willingness to compromise, establish trust, engage in honest conversation, etc., can make or break the mediation process. This dynamic is vividly illustrated in the Mahabharata, where Duryodhana's rigid stance and refusal to concede any territory exemplify how inflexibility can doom mediation efforts.

Similar patterns are evident in modern geopolitical conflicts such as the Israeli-Palestinian conflict or the Russia-Ukraine war, where entrenched positions and deep-seated mistrust often lead to a breakdown of negotiations. These examples show that the attitude of the parties involved is a decisive factor in determining whether the mediation leads to a peaceful resolution or collapses into conflict, highlighting their crucial role in the success or failure of mediation.

III. Mediating with the Mahabharata — An Overview

The Mahabharata is an ancient Indian epic that narrates the story of two cousin groups, the Kauravas, the hundred sons of King Dhritarashtra; and the Pandavas, the five sons of King Pandu. Both factions held legitimate claims to the throne. At the heart of the conflict was the fact that the Kauravas ruled over the entire kingdom, with Hastinapur as the capital, and refused to grant even five villages to the Pandavas.

To facilitate a clearer understanding of the dynamics, below are the tables detailing the mediator (Table 1), the parties involved (Table 2), and the relationships mentioned throughout the essay (Table 3), which aim to provide a clear overview of the interaction and roles within the narrative and the mediation.

Lord Krishna, the most respectable, revered, and sought-after guidance persona throughout the Bharatvarsha (the Indian subcontinent), was uniquely positioned to mediate between these two powerful parties to avert catastrophic conflict. Yudhishtira, the eldest among the Pandavas,

Table 1

The Mediator	
Lord Krishna	An avatar of Vishnu and a relative to both parties

Table 2

The Parties			
The Kauravas (Hundred sons of King Dhritarashtra)		**The Pandavas (Five sons of King Pandu)**	
Duryodhana	Eldest among the Kauravas, Prince of Kuru Kingdom and the representative of his party	Yudhishtira	Eldest among the Pandavas and the representative of his party
Dushasana	Second eldest among the Kauravas and the younger brother of Duryodhana	Arjuna	The third of the Pandava brothers
The rest	The remaining 98 brothers	Bhima, Nakul, Sahdev	Rest of the brothers

Table 3

Other Characters' relationship with the Parties involved in the Mediation	
Bhishma	Grandfather of both the Pandavas and Kauravas
Drona	Guru (Teacher) or royal preceptor of both the Pandavas and the Kauravas
Dhritarashtra	The King of the Kuru Kingdom, father of the Kauravas and paternal uncle of the Pandavas
Draupadi	The neutral wife of all five of the Pandava brothers
Karna	Half-brother to the Pandavas and a loyal friend of Duryodhana. He saw Arjuna as his competitor
Pandu	Father of the Pandavas and paternal uncle of the Kauravas
Shakuni	Maternal uncle of the Kauravas
Vidura	Paternal uncle of both the Pandavas and Kauravas

approached Lord Krishna and informed him about his uncle's and cousin's intentions. He explained to Lord Krishna that the Kauravas had denied his request for a mere five villages to secure a peaceful resolution. Yudhishtira expressed his unwillingness to fight against his family members. He implored Lord Krishna to visit Hastinapur as "shantidoot" (a mediator) and mediate the dispute between them and the Kauravas.

Lord Krishna agreed to mediate and left for Hastinapur to meet the Kauravas. When Dhritarashtra learnt about Lord Krishna's impending visit, he advised Duryodhana to be present for the mediation to impress Lord Krishna in every possible way so that he would side with them. Duryodhana agreed to the mediation. Later on, Duryodhana revealed his vicious intention to detain Lord Krishna if forced to give a share of the kingdom to the Pandavas. He was well aware that if he succeeded in his attempt to confine Lord Krishna, it would ultimately lead to the Pandavas' surrender.

During the mediation, Lord Krishna initiated the negotiation and productive dialogue, successfully persuading Dhritarashtra to give the Pandavas their share, but Duryodhana resisted. Lord Krishna, Dhritarashtra, Bhishma, Drona and Vidur attempted to reason with Duryodhana, but he refused to concede. He attempted to confine Lord Krishna and failed. This action of Duryodhana resulted in the breakdown of mediation and a war.

IV. Parties' Influence and Outcome of Mediation

The characters within the epic at the time of mediation represent diverse attitudes, behaviours, and strategies, each impacting the success or failure of mediation attempts. By examining parties' influence, we can gain a deeper understanding of mediation outcomes as we navigate conflicts and negotiations.

A. *The intention of the parties*

The Pandavas had a genuine desire to resolve the conflict and establish peace. On the other hand, Duryodhana had malicious intentions, showing no interest in having an honest conversation or mediating. His only goal behind participating in the mediation was the possibility of being able to confine Lord Krishna so that he could make the Pandavas helpless and force them to surrender. The situation conveys a significant meaning — if parties such as Duryodhana lack genuine desire to negotiate in good faith, the efforts of the mediator and the other party become irrelevant, ultimately influencing the outcome of the mediation negatively.

For instance, the Iran nuclear deal of 2015 was a success because of the genuine intention of the parties involved. Iran's sincere intention to lift the sanctions and the P5+1 countries' willingness to prevent nuclear proliferation led to the successful agreement. On the other hand, the current mediation efforts between Israel and Hamas in Gaza often falter due to the conflicting intentions of the parties. While international mediators seek to broker ceasefires and long-term peace agreements, the intentions of Hamas are often seen as ambiguous. Thus, the intention of the parties significantly influences the mediation outcomes.

B. *Willingness of parties to compromise*

Duryodhana was clearly unwilling to compromise. Although the Pandavas had a legitimate claim to have an equal share in the kingdom, they demanded only five villages in the hopes of achieving a peaceful settlement. However, Duryodhana arrogantly declared that the Pandavas would not be given "a needlepoint of land as long as he was alive".[2] Duryodhana's attitude hindered the mediation process, as mediation often requires parties to compromise to reach a mutually acceptable resolution.

Parties unwilling to make a compromise or concession or consider the interest of other parties often prevent a satisfactory outcome in mediation. A parallel can be drawn with the ongoing Kashmir conflict between India and Pakistan. The dispute continues to be unresolved because both nations have historically shown minimal willingness to compromise on territorial claims and governance issues. It has ultimately led to a series of wars and the destruction of lives.

C. *Lack of trust in the mediator*

Duryodhana had never trusted Lord Krishna, believing that Lord Krishna was biased against the Kauravas and favoured the Pandavas. However, Lord Krishna maintained that he was neutral and sought to mediate for both parties, aiming to resolve the dispute and avoid war. This impartial stance is further reinforced in Srimad Bhagavad Gita, where Lord Krishna said: "I envy no one nor am I partial to anyone; I am equal to all".[3] Duryodhana's lack of trust in Lord Krishna led the outcome of the mediation to be negative. This significantly shows us that despite the mediator's skills, expertise and desire to resolve the conflict on a positive note, if parties do not trust the mediator, the process is unlikely to succeed.

A contemporary example of mediation can be seen in the Syrian Civil War, where the UN attempted to mediate. The lack of success could be attributed to mistrust, as the Syrians perceive the UN as being unable to effectively challenge the Assad regime or protect their interest, partly due to the influence of Russia, a key ally of Assad, within the UN Security Council. This mistrust has led to multiple failed peace talks.

D. *Adversarial behaviour*

Throughout the mediation process, Duryodhana was exhibiting confrontational rather than cooperative behaviour. He engaged in personal attacks, created conspiracies about Lord Krishna and tried to confine him. These actions escalated the matter and undermined the effectiveness of the mediation process.

Parties who adopt such adversarial behaviour during the mediation process create a hostile environment obstructing the dispute settlement. In the modern context, parties may sometimes engage in such adversarial behaviour in the heat of the moment, and cross boundaries, which can set back the mediation process significantly. It is essential not to engage in adversarial behaviour for a satisfactory outcome.

E. *Commitment of parties to resolve the dispute*

The Pandavas consistently demonstrated a commitment to resolving the conflict. They were the first ones to approach Lord Krishna for mediation. In contrast, Duryodhana showcased a lack of commitment to resolve the conflict. If parties do not intend to settle the dispute, mediation is futile.

A contemporary example can be seen in the Colombian peace process between the Colombian government and the Revolutionary Armed Forces of Colombia ("**FARC**"). For decades, peace talks had failed due to a lack of genuine commitment from both sides to resolve the dispute. However, in 2016, both parties showed a renewed and sincere commitment to the peace process, leading to a successful agreement. The government demonstrated the commitment to resolve the conflict by addressing social and economic issues that fuelled the conflict, while FARC agreed to disarm and transform into a political party.

This mutual commitment is essential in reaching sustainable solutions. When parties express genuine commitment to finding a resolution, they engage more constructively and actively in the mediation. Conversely, if parties lack commitment, they may resist cooperation and productive communication, and by doing so impede the progress of the mediation.

F. *Respect for the process*

Duryodhana's attempt to confine Lord Krishna during the ongoing negotiations and his refusal to heed Lord Krishna's counsel reflected a lack of respect for the mediation process and the mediator's authority. He consistently disregarded the process when it did not align with his personal ambitions for power and control. His lack of respect for peaceful resolutions and his inclination to use force hindered efforts to achieve a diplomatic settlement.

Parties involved in mediation should respect the mediation process and the role of the mediator in guiding negotiation and facilitating discussions. This includes refraining from engaging in any disruptive and disrespectful behaviours and abiding by the decision of the mediation.

The Yemen Civil War is an example of parties showing disrespect for the mediation. The Houthi rebels and the Saudi-led coalition have repeatedly violated ceasefire agreements brokered by UN mediators. These violations undermine the credibility of the mediation process and erode trust between parties, making it difficult to sustain meaningful negotiations. Without a foundation of respect for the mediator and the process, the mediation becomes a fruitless exercise, wasting the time and effort of everyone involved.

G. *History between the parties*

The relationship between the Pandavas and the Kauravas had been full of conflicts. Duryodhana's quest for power and control, and deep-seated resentment and jealousy towards the Pandavas made him resort to using underhanded tactics and fuelling conspiracies against them. The Pandavas had been humiliated and unfairly treated — there was the poisoning of Bhima, the construction of a lacquer house (Lakshagraha) meant to trap and burn them alive, and the infamous manipulation of a gambling match. In this rigged dice game, Yudhisthir was deceived into wagering his kingdom, wealth, and even his brothers, his wife Draupadi and himself. Following the loss, Duryodhana and his brothers publicly humiliated Draupadi. Dushasana, on the order of Duryodhana, attempted to disrobe Draupadi in an assembly hall in full view of the courtiers and elders present. These incidents led to the Pandavas' subsequent exile for 13 years.

Despite the grave injustices suffered by the Pandavas and cruelty perpetrated by the Kauravas, the Pandavas demonstrated a willingness to move beyond these past conflicts for the sake of peace. Despite their rightful claim being denied and years of exile and humiliation, they pursued mediation as a peaceful means to resolve the conflict.

The history between parties significantly impacts the success or failure of a mediation, particularly if it is tainted by past conflict. This is evident when looking at the dynamic between North Korea and South Korea, which is deeply influenced by their history, dating back to the Division of Korea (1945) and the Korean War (1950–1953).

Despite diplomatic efforts, unresolved grievances and the shadow of past conflicts often lead to the rehashing of old issues and impede progress towards peace resolution. There were hopes for peace after the 2018 summit, but these faded quickly during the communication breakdown of 2020 and subsequent provocations, like the recent launch of rubbish-filled balloons.

The same thing can also be seen in the Israeli-Palestinian conflict — the 1948 Arab-Israeli War, the Six-Day War in 1967, and subsequent intifadas (uprisings). These deep historical scars are often the reason for ongoing hostility.'

Unresolved grievances or lingering resentments impact current negotiations. Instead of focussing on rehashing old arguments, it is imperative that parties cooperate or compromise so that they can look forward to finding constructive solutions. If parties can acknowledge and move beyond past conflicts, it will increase the likelihood of reaching a successful mediation outcome.

H. *Power dynamics*

The Kauravas, being in a position of power, were not motivated to settle. As the ruling faction with control over the kingdom of Hastinapur, the Kauravas enjoyed significant political and military power. This position of dominance gave them the confidence to dictate their terms rather than negotiate. This political dominance diminished their incentive to engage in meaningful mediation efforts and made the Kauravas, especially Duryodhana, overconfident in their ability to achieve victory through force. As such, they were unwilling to compromise and viewed the mediation as unnecessary or futile.

Also, when pressurised by mediators like Lord Krishna and elders like Bhishma to seek reconciliation, Duryodhana's powerful position allowed him to resist. Power dynamics significantly influence mediation outcomes, as the relative power and the influence of the parties involved shape their willingness to engage in the process and their negotiation approach. In many contemporary conflicts, such as those in the Middle East and Eastern Europe, geopolitical interests and regional rivalries create complex power dynamics that influence mediation outcomes.

I. *Unrealistic expectations and demands from parties*

The Pandavas' demand for only five villages as a settlement offer exemplified a pragmatic and realistic approach. However, the Kauravas rejected this modest proposal, which reflected their desire for total control and dominance. This ultimately obstructed any chance of a successful mediation and escalated tensions into a full-scale war at Kurukshetra. Realistic or unrealistic expectations by parties significantly influence the outcome of mediation.

In international conflicts, countries show unrealistic expectations when they demand maximum concession or positions for the settlement.

They should set realistic expectations by considering the interests of other parties and make acceptable and reasonable demands. If parties set unrealistic expectations, they should not be surprised to find a negative mediation outcome and no end to the conflict in sight.

J. *External influences*

Duryodhana's foremost advisors, Karna and Shakuni, played a crucial role in shaping Duryodhana's attitude towards mediation, because of the way they encouraged him to take a hardline stance. Karna, driven by a personal agenda to prove himself superior to Arjuna, consistently validated of Duryodhana's views and decisions, no matter how extreme, which made Duryodhana feel more confident and made him uncompromising in his position. Karna believed in the Kshatriya duty of combat and valour and saw compromise as a weakness. He passed this perspective on to Duryodhana, discouraging reconciliation.

Shakuni was the maternal uncle of Duryodhana and closest to him. He was a master manipulator and strategist in the Mahabharata who encouraged aggressive and uncompromising tactics and advised Duryodhana to use force and intimidation rather than diplomacy. He influenced Duryodhana, leading to the latter's rejection of peaceful solutions. The influence of Karna and Shakuni on Duryodhana illustrates the broader principle that the attitudes, advice, and actions of involved parties and their influential advisers are critical determinants of mediation outcomes.

Managing such influences is essential for mediators. However, parties should also be responsible for evaluating such influences, which can derail negotiations and escalate disputes into open conflict. For instance, the conflict in Syria has been heavily influenced by external parties, such as the United States, Russia, Iran and Turkey. These countries have backed different factions within Syria, motivated by their own strategic interests, complicating mediation efforts led by the UN and international bodies. Rather than facilitating a peaceful resolution, these external influences have deepened divisions, exacerbating the conflict.

V. Conclusion

The Mahabharata's lessons on mediation remain strikingly relevant in today's world. It emphasises that the success of mediation largely hinges on the attitude and actions of the involved parties. It teaches us that mediation is not a process but a delicate art that requires more than a mediator's skills, demanding the commitment to peace and respect of all parties involved.

As observed in contemporary conflicts such as those in Syria and between Israel and Palestine, the failure to align the intentions and respect the mediation process often leads to continued strife and missed opportunities for peace. As we strive to mediate modern disputes, it becomes imperative to reflect on both ancient epics and contemporary examples, fostering an environment where peace and collaboration can prevail over discord and division.

https://doi.org/10.1142/9789819825042_0005

Chapter 5

Unravelling Neutrality: Examining Neutrality as a Core Mediation Principle in Facilitative and Evaluative Mediation Models

Lee En Jia Chloe

I. Introduction

Neutrality has become synonymous with the essence of mediation: It is taught in mediation courses, and mediation has been described as a process with a neutral third party in the majority of academic literature. This principle has often been featured in discussions on mediator standards and ethics, and now seems to have become a cornerstone of what it means to be a mediator. Consequently, this has repercussions on party expectations, as well as the process and conduct of a mediator.

This paper thus seeks to unravel neutrality. Firstly, I will examine the role of neutrality as a mediation principle in the classic facilitative and evaluative mediation models. Secondly, I challenge the assumption that neutrality is inherently relevant in mediation, and argue that it is not necessarily a fundamental cornerstone in mediation. Additionally, to add another dimension to this discussion, the divide between facilitative and evaluative mediation seems more theoretical than practical. This means that a more holistic approach moving forward is necessary, as it is more meaningful to discuss neutrality in relation to specific skills instead of through a binary lens of facilitative and evaluative mediation.

II. Defining Key Terms

As a preliminary step, it is important to define the concept of neutrality. Neutrality is often used in conjunction with impartiality. Typically, academic literature distinguishes between neutrality and impartiality. Neutrality refers to a disinterestedness in the outcome of the dispute and the absence of real and perceived conflicts of interest in relation to a matter.[1,2] According to Australian mediation standards, impartiality refers to a sense of fairness, including the way the process is conducted and how parties are treated.[3] For the purposes of this paper, I will adopt Astor's definition of neutrality, as a concept interchangeable with impartiality[4] and which comprises several elements.

Firstly, the mediator does not influence the content of the outcome of mediation. Secondly, the mediator is not partisan and will treat the parties equally, not favouring one over the other. Thirdly, the mediator should not be influenced by financial or personal connection with the disputants, and should be aware of prejudicial information about either or both of the parties. Fourthly, the mediator should be free from influence by governments. Lastly, the mediator should have independence, as canvassed in the third and fourth elements to maintain mediator neutrality.

III. How Does Neutrality Feature in Facilitative Mediation?

Neutrality features strongly in facilitative mediation. Briefly, this paper will reference Riskin's grid that explains the facilitative, evaluative, broad and narrow mediation models, with a particular focus on the facilitative-evaluative dichotomy.

Based on Riskin's definition of a facilitative mediator, it is inappropriate for the mediator to give opinions for two reasons. Firstly, offering opinions might affect the appearance of impartiality and interfere with the mediator's ability to function. Secondly, the mediator may lack sufficient knowledge or details of the case to give an informed opinion.[5] Facilitative mediation encompasses a mediator focussing more on a party's need and interests, assisting by providing neutrality and objectivity to allow parties to understand each other.[6,7] Therefore, it is apparent that neutrality seems to be a cornerstone of the facilitative mediator's principles.

In fact, mediators are often known as neutral third parties who help disputants come to a consensus on their own.[8] Neutrality is so significant to the facilitative mediator's role that the terms "mediator" and "neutral" are sometimes used interchangeably.[9] This manifests in the expectation that facilitative mediators must act in a neutral and impartial way in relation to the parties throughout the mediation process.[10] This conduct would involve using neutral verbal language throughout the whole process, such as when paraphrasing parties' common interests and differences, framing issues, and even ensuring that the body language adopted is neutral.

In line with facilitative mediation, neutrality encourages parties to share openly about their interests and perspectives thereby aiding the interest-gathering stage of mediation. Looking at the current Singapore International Mediation Institute ("**SIMI**") Competency Framework for Mediators, where SIMI recognises facilitative mediation as being commonly regarded to be the most mainstream form of mediation, "neutrality" is included as a Relationship Management component under the List of Core Competencies.[11] This further strengthens the argument that neutrality features strongly in facilitative mediation.

IV. How Does Neutrality Feature in Evaluative Mediation?

Coben presents the view that evaluative mediation has borrowed concepts of neutrality due to the increasing adoption of mediation in more evaluative settings. The increased institutionalisation and court-annexation has "dramatically influenced" mediation with "legal and judicial concepts of impartiality and concerns about conflicts of interest".[12] Therefore, his argument stems from a historical perspective where neutrality is most often defined as the obligation for mediators to act with impartiality, which is in turn defined as the "freedom from favouritism or bias in word, action or appearance, and includ[ing] a commitment to assist all participants as opposed to any one individual".[13]

On the other hand, there are critics of Riskin's grid, arguing that evaluative mediation may not be compatible with the principle of neutrality. This is because evaluative mediators tend to give an opinion or assessment of the strength or weakness of parties' cases, which Chua argued jeopardises mediator neutrality by invariably favouring one side over the other.[14] Kovach and Love highlight that evaluative activities may "shut down the mediation process" because such evaluative settings typically promote an adversarial climate without parties trying to understand each other's interests.[15] Parties instead try to convince the neutral third party of their respective arguments, and only a mediator who remains neutral will be able to use the tools of facilitated negotiation, such as encouraging parties to discern their underlying concerns and engage in creative problem-solving.[16]

An example would include Hong Kong, where the evaluative mediation model has been promoted by the government in intellectual property ("**IP**") disputes for expert advisory mediations.[17] A mediator in this case would be an IP expert who possesses authority through expertise, and is likely to give an assessment of the case merits, potentially coming across as being biased. Parties would also have expected mediation in this context to be more directive, thereby relegating neutrality as a principle to the backseat.

In spite of neutrality seeming to feature less in evaluative mediation, mediator codes seem to refer to neutrality as a universal principle in both models. For example, the Olé! Case Evaluation Tool is an analysis and evaluation tool used by the International Mediation Institute ("**IMI**") to help analyse mediation disputes and determine the best way forward. It differentiates facilitative from evaluative mediation. While evaluative mediation helps the parties to "understand objective parameters based on which an outcome would be reached using specific norms", facilitative mediation "helps [parties] to elicit their respective interests" to reach a mutually acceptable settlement based on their subjective and future interests.[18]

V. Is the Assumption that Neutrality is an Indispensable Mediation Principle True?

Much ink has been spilt over neutrality losing its place as a key mediation principle due to two reasons. First, it is difficult or impossible for any mediator to be completely neutral. Second, it is not always desirable for mediators to be neutral, as much depends on the context of mediation.

A. *Is being neutral feasible?*

A strong argument for neutrality being unfeasible is the impracticability for a mediator to "exclude personal opinions" and therefore be "absolutely neutral".[19] This view is affirmed by Jones and Hughes, who argued that mediators are actually co-participants in the conflict, and inevitably bring their own unspoken and often unrecognised biases to the conflict. This biased viewpoint should be embraced in order to begin constructively engaging in the conflict with the parties — which also relates to the next section on desirability.[20] In sum, mediators always influence the content and outcome, no matter how strongly one claims to be completely objective and neutral.[21]

Mayer also argued that neutrality may be a disingenuous separation between active listening and genuine empathy. This is because neutrality may translate into mediators appearing indifferent, unengaged, unsupportive, or inattentive, which may seem antithetical to a mediator's role to actively listen to the parties.[22] However, it is my view that with sufficient experience and tact, it is possible for mediators to exhibit neutral conduct, while still being engaged and supportive.

Neutrality may also be a tricky principle in the context of mediation funded by third parties. There may potentially be conflicts of interest, although this has been canvassed more so in arbitration than mediation.[23] Since third-party funders decide on funding after considering the likelihood of success and recovery of monies, it is difficult for mediators to be completely disinterested in the outcome.[24] In that sense, Mayer argued that mediators are accountable to whoever funded the mediation, and therefore cannot be said to be truly neutral in the outcome.[25]

A notable example is the successful Camp David negotiations in 1978 where Egyptian President Anwar Sadat and Israeli Prime Minister Menachem Begin drafted a "Framework for Peace in the Middle East".[26] In this instance, the President of the United States, Jimmy Carter, who brokered this agreement, was not a neutral mediator as he had to represent the interests of the US. His "stake" or "non-neutrality" at the mediation table meant that he had a great deal of resources to incentivise the parties to reach an agreement, or conversely, impose sanctions on them for non-compliance.

B. *Is being neutral desirable?*

Desmond Tutu ("**Tutu**"), a South African archbishop and human rights activist summarises the desirability of neutrality in a quote: "If you are neutral in situations of injustice, you have chosen the side of the oppressor. If an elephant has its foot on the tail of a mouse and you say that you are neutral, the mouse will not appreciate your neutrality."[27]

An obvious qualifier to Tutu's statement is that not all mediations take place in situations of injustice. However, the statement holds true for quite a number of mediation contexts. In an Asian context, an "insider" mediator is more favourably looked upon because of the stronger relational orientation where parties and mediator share connections or commonalities, which may earn them more trust and influence. Conversely, a neutral third party with no prior relationship with the parties would be relegated to an "out-group member to be dealt with at arm's length".[28] Lee argued that a stronger relational orientation benefits the mediation process by helping to pave the way for a resolution as parties will be put at ease and will be more motivated to act reasonably and also adopt a "give-and-take" attitude. Sharp also endorsed this view that connectedness to parties may be more important than adopting a neutral approach to mediation.[29]

Further from Asia, this view was also echoed. A study done on 30 US mediators from 2003 to 2005 found that three-quarters of the mediators surveyed emphasised developing rapport with the parties. This emphasised a mediator's innate ability to connect with the parties, and those surveyed opined that trust and rapport mattered the most as a key element in successful mediation.[30] Rapport would presumably be built easily if the mediator has established relations with the parties.

An example includes the Navajo peacemakers, who commenced their peacemaking process by declaring their clan affiliations and continued until everyone involved had declared their affiliations.[31] This approach is the opposite of selecting a mediator who is neutral in the sense of being unaffiliated. Therefore, this example, among many other cultural examples, shows that accepted mediators are often people with standing in the community such as elders, religious leaders, governmental officials or others who are respected for their positions as opposed to being respected for their neutrality or mediation experience.[32] This was put succinctly by

Meera Rajah, who argued that there will almost always be inherent suspicion vis-à-vis the mediator's neutrality.[33] Considering the examples, I agree insofar as the cultural context calls for connected or related mediators.

Lastly, Mayer also argued that conflicting parties may at times want something other than neutral intervention. They may seek opportunities for voice, justice, vindication, validation and impact when they are in a conflict.[34] In this way, neutrality is actually counter-intuitive and may impede the process of mediation.

In summary, neutrality does not seem to be desirable in a number of mediation contexts based on the academic literature. This is surprising given the emphasis on neutrality in setting party expectations, in how mediators are assessed and more.

VI. Distinguishing Between Facilitative and Evaluative Mediation

In any case, there seems to be an arbitrary distinction between facilitative and evaluative mediation. There is an age-old dichotomy between facilitative and evaluative mediation, which in recent times has seemed to meld into less of a binary inquiry. It is important to examine if core mediation principles such as neutrality, as seen in codes of conduct for mediators, feature similarly in both mediation styles. This analysis would have an impact on the way mediation is conducted and helps to establish norms and expectations for both mediators and parties alike.

It is notable that many other jurisdictions have adopted an inclusive and diverse range of mediation models. For example, the National Mediator Standards in Australia are based on a facilitative mediation model, but recognise diversity in practice as blended processes.[35] Singapore's accreditation body, SIMI, also recognises Asian approaches to mediation, while the Singapore International Dispute Resolution Academy provides training in diverse culturally fluent mediation models.[36]

As highlighted earlier, the seemingly dichotomous divide between facilitative and evaluative mediation is as such: Facilitative mediation encompasses a mediator focussing more on a party's needs and interests and the mediator assists by providing neutrality and objectivity to allow parties to understand each other[37]; on the other hand, evaluative mediation involves the mediator evaluating the likely outcome to persuade parties towards a compromised solution. It is assumed the parties want and need the mediator to provide guidance through the person's training, experience and objectivity.

However, most scholars are sceptical of this divide. Academics also argue that it is impossible for a purely facilitative mediation to take place, given the varying manner and degree in which evaluative mediation is conducted, coupled with the practical realities of mediation.[38] This is especially so for commercial disputes, where the term "facilitating the evaluation" has been coined for such cases.[39] In practice, mediators also often use an amalgamation of methods, and both methods are in fact, inseparable.[40,41] For example, one may commence with facilitative methods to better gather party interests, but subsequently adopt a more evaluative approach to direct parties towards settlement.[42]

VII. Moving Forward

Several academics have also proposed ways to circumvent mediator neutrality, or ways to frame the role of a mediator more accurately. William Ury proposed that mediators should take "the Third Side". His proposition does not necessitate the mediator taking a neutral stance. Instead, he argued that a mediator should seek to understand both sides of the conflict, which goes further than being absolutely neutral, albeit having natural sympathies for one side.[43]

A similar proposal includes the principle of omnipartiality, which Cloke introduces in *Mediating Dangerously: The Frontiers of Conflict Resolution*. This means to speak, listen, and behave as though we were on both sides of the dispute, instead of none at all.[44]

Given the practical difficulties of the dichotomy, I agree with Chua in arguing that it would be more apposite to avoid focussing on defining what mediation is, but instead examine specific mediation techniques that a mediator can employ depending on the context. Neutrality may not feature strongly for situations when the mediator is giving an opinion, reality testing or using power to encourage settlement because it would be impossible for both sides to weigh equally in terms of the argument, and this would depend on how realistic their proposals are.

However, neutrality may remain valuable when one is proposing solutions or re-framing the conversation such that both parties feel involved, so that the dialogue and contributions are equally distributed between them.[45]

https://doi.org/10.1142/9789819825042_0006

Chapter 6

Two Pieces of a Puzzle: A Collaborative Reading of the Singapore Convention and the New York Convention

Meghna Jandu

I. Introduction

Can the Singapore Convention be regarded as the New York Convention equivalent for international mediation? Both treaties, the United Nations Convention on International Settlement Agreements Resulting from Mediation ("**Singapore Convention**") and the Convention on the Recognition and Enforcement of Foreign Arbitral Awards ("**New York Convention**"), provide frameworks for the international enforcement of the outcome of a dispute resolution process.

Both conventions contribute to the strengthening of the system of private international law. Drawing on this simplistic understanding, the answer to the above question appears to be "yes". The following parts of this paper explore the complexities of this question to further the view that the two conventions must be viewed as two pieces of the same puzzle: that in international dispute resolution, one cannot replace the other. However, putting the first piece in place can aid in the correct placement of the second.

The arguments advanced in this paper address the oft-quoted concern of why the Singapore Convention was needed in the first place. The first part of this paper addresses this concern as it delves into the text and background of the Singapore Convention to highlight its unique purpose within the international private law framework. The second part of this paper addresses the practical concerns that users of mediation face in utilising the Singapore Convention to enforce an international mediated settlement agreement (“**international settlement agreement**” or “**settlement agreement**”).

The argument is that while the Singapore Convention is still nascent, this does not mean it should be parked aside till it gains greater acceptance, an argument put forward by some.[1] It is argued that the New York Convention can be utilised to expand the use of mediation, as a status quo bias operating in favour of arbitration. The discussion highlights one particularly useful way that the arbitration regime can be utilised to further the use of mediation in international commercial disputes.

II. Tracing the Need for the Singapore Convention

During its 63rd session in 2015, the United Nations Commission on International Trade Law (“**UNCITRAL**”) Working Group II (“**WG II**”) commenced its deliberations on the need to draft an instrument that would strengthen the regime of cross-border enforcement of international settlement agreements. Towards the end of that session, it was agreed that an international convention should be drafted to enforce settlement agreements.[2] The WG II’s deliberations over subsequent sessions reflect on the gaps that the new instrument would be drafted to address, highlighting the unique position that such an instrument would hold within the international private law framework.

Firstly, WG II recognised that there was a need to draft an international legal instrument that would specifically be tailored to provide for the enforcement of settlement agreements obtained through the “flexible” mode of mediation (notably, the term “conciliation” was more frequently used instead of “mediation” in the initial deliberations of the WG II. This paper uses the term “mediation” for consistency).

Secondly, the need to aid parties who are keen on using mediation to enforce settlement agreements through a dedicated convention was also recognised by the WG II. The discussions frequently referred to the other existing international instruments which may overlap with the scope of the new instrument. Ultimately, the Singapore Convention reflects a concerted effort to draft a specialised, separate instrument for mediated settlement agreements to be enforced internationally.

A. *To preserve the flexibility of mediation*

The WG II intended to cater to users of mediation, who preferred to use this process of dispute resolution for its flexibility. It was largely agreed that the flexible nature of mediation made it distinct from other modes of dispute resolution, and this defining feature needed to be preserved and provided for in the new instrument. The discussions of the WG II on "form and other requirements of settlement agreements" shed light on the need to preserve the flexible nature of the mediation process.[3]

While there was general agreement that a settlement agreement should be in writing, it was agreed that the form requirement of such a settlement agreement need not be overly prescriptive.[4] As a result, the drafting of Article 4 of the Convention reflects fairly straightforward form requirements: that the settlement agreement must be signed by the parties, and that there must be evidence that the settlement agreement resulted from mediation.

Such evidence may be in the form of (i) the signature of the mediator on the agreement, (ii) a document signed by the mediator confirming that mediation had taken place, or (iii) a similar attestation from the mediation institution, if involved. Lastly, in the absence of (i), (ii) or (iii), any other evidence that may be acceptable to the enforcing authority further enhances flexibility.[5]

It was also agreed by the WG II that unlike the New York Convention, which provides for "recognition" and "enforcement" of arbitral awards, the Singapore Convention need not provide for recognition separate from enforcement. The *travaux préparatoires* makes clear that this choice was made in an effort to streamline the enforcement process. One motivation for this was to reduce complications and avoid delayed enforcement by giving an extra layer of determination to the enforcing authority. Furthermore, it was also not intended that any *res judicata* effect should be given to settlement agreements obtained through mediation, in the manner that arbitral awards are given this effect.[6]

B. *To establish a distinct enforcement mechanism for international settlement agreements*

The intention to provide for a distinct international instrument that is well suited to be utilised for mediation is clearly captured in the preamble of the Singapore Convention. The last recital of the preamble states that parties to the convention are convinced that there is a need for such a framework which would be acceptable to states with differing legal, social and economic systems and that the same would aid in furthering and harmonising states' international economic relations.[7]

Even as references were frequently made to the prevailing New York Convention and the 2005 Hague Convention on the Choice of Court Agreements, the issue of overlap with these instruments also arose time and again. In fact, the matter was covered in detail during the discussion on the agenda of "Settlement agreements reached during judicial or arbitral proceedings".[8] During discussions over this agenda, the question of covering those settlement agreements that would be enforceable as consent arbitral awards or judgments within the new instrument, came up. It was noted that such inclusion may have a propensity of overlap between the new instrument and the existing instruments, such as the New York Convention.

Another concern raised in this regard was that by covering such settlement agreements, multiple instruments would apply to a single text.[9] For instance, if a settlement is arrived at in the course of arbitration, would it then be covered by the Singapore Convention or the New York Convention?

While the text of the Singapore Convention carefully avoids this overlap by excluding settlement agreements that are recorded as judgments or arbitral awards, it is important to note that the Convention includes settlement agreements reached during judicial or arbitration proceedings but <u>not</u> recorded as an order of court or a consent award.[10] To this extent, it is clear that the Singapore Convention fills a gap: settlements formed during arbitral or judicial processes that were not formalised now benefit from the Singapore Convention. This offers further support to the idea that the intention was to segregate the application of each of these separate legal instruments.

In addition to the deliberations of the WG II and the text of the Singapore Convention, the *travaux préparatoires* of the New York Convention support the position posited above that the Singapore Convention and the New York Convention serve two distinct purposes. In that regard, it is worth highlighting that during the drafting of the New York Convention, Austria had proposed an amendment to Article 1 of the New York Convention to the effect that the Convention should also apply to arbitral settlements.[11] The fact that the New York Convention rejected the amendment further bolsters the suggestion that the intention of the New York Convention was meant solely for the enforcement of arbitral awards and not settlement agreements. As a result, the Singapore Convention was necessitated to provide a mechanism to enforce settlement agreements internationally.

III. Reception of the Singapore Convention

After much deliberation and detailed discussions, the Singapore Convention opened for signing on August 7, 2019. At the time, the Convention received historically unprecedented sign-ups on the first day, with several major economies supporting and signing the Convention. However, it received lukewarm responses in terms of ratification over the subsequent years. As of June 2025, 58 countries have signed the Convention, including major Asian and global economies such as the United States of America, China, the United Kingdom and India. However, only 18 countries have so far ratified the Convention, with the biggest economy being Japan, which ratified the Convention only in October 2023 and the Convention coming into effect there on April 2024. By contrast, the New York Convention is one of the most successful international instruments, with nearly 172 state parties having ratified the Convention.

The Singapore Convention has come to be viewed as a laudable initiative to put mediation on the map as a meaningful tool for resolution of cross-border disputes and as a credible acknowledgement of mediation.[12] However, the ultimate success of the Singapore Convention now rests with the states that have yet to ratify and sign it. As greater numbers of countries sign the Singapore Convention, mediation in the international landscape will gain traction.[13]

However, at the moment, given scarce ratification, parties wishing to enforce mediated settlements internationally often find that they are unable to avail themselves of the benefits of the Singapore Convention. This has not only resulted in the Singapore Convention not yet being able to attain its intended objective, but has also led to mediation becoming less popular as a mode of dispute resolution. The question of how a settlement agreement will be enforced internationally continues to loom large in discussions on mediation.

IV. Finding a Solution to the Enforcement Dilemma

Even though mediated settlement agreements have a strong compliance rate,[14] parties often seek to enter into an agreement that they can enforce through a formal mechanism. This is often the case in cross-border transactions, where parties may not have had a long-standing commercial relationship, and as such there may be little to no trust that their counterpart will comply with the terms of the agreement. In such cases, parties are less likely to use mediation when the enforcement process is not robust.

So where does this leave us? Should parties abandon the idea of mediation until more countries sign the Singapore Convention? This would be a pity, considering all the progress made by the proponents of mediation, practitioners and academics alike.

It is suggested that until the Singapore Convention gains greater acceptance, parties should continue to utilise the New York Convention to enforce settlement agreements as arbitral awards. This strategy would serve two important purposes. Firstly, it will allow for the growth of mediation by utilising the status quo bias that operates in favour of arbitration. Secondly, it will allow parties to use mediation, while also having the assurance of nearly worldwide enforcement through the New York Convention.

A. *The advantageous position of arbitration*

One reason many states hesitate to ratify the Singapore Convention is due to an information deficit concerning mediation. Countries may not see value in supporting a mode of dispute resolution that disputants seldom use. Equally, there is an information deficit regarding the usefulness of mediation even amongst legal practitioners, thereby contributing to its relatively rare uptake by parties. No doubt the lack of a strong enforcement mechanism also contributes to mediation's scarce uptake. This is a vicious cycle, and it is proposed that leveraging arbitration to promote mediation might be able to break this cycle.

As opposed to mediation, arbitration as a mode of dispute resolution enjoys "information abundance". The New York Convention, the UNCITRAL Model Law on International Commercial Arbitration (1985; revised in 2006) and every arbitration legislation in the world has received fairly adequate attention. This may be through courts' interpretation of the text of an instrument or through academic commentaries on every provision of these instruments.

Additionally, engagement efforts by arbitral institutions and lawyers with focussed arbitration practice have contributed to the growth of knowledge in the field of arbitration. A link may be drawn between the expansive knowledge of the process of arbitration and its default uptake by parties and inclusion of this process within contracts by lawyers.

To propose a shift from this default, influence may be drawn from the experience of arbitration breaking the "status quo bias" operating in favour of litigation. "Status quo bias" arises when individuals or institutions prefer an "established course of action over any available alternatives, even if those alternatives would increase the welfare of the decision maker".[15] A full analysis of the "status quo bias" operating in favour of arbitration requires a much more detailed discussion and is beyond the scope of this paper.

Nonetheless, the stronghold of arbitration is evident in the international dispute resolution landscape. Until a more efficient mode of dispute resolution comes about, this stronghold is unlikely to weaken. Mediation may well be that mode of dispute resolution, taking into account its unique benefits, which include the preservation of business relationships, confidentiality and speed.[16]

It is thus suggested that as the information gap about mediation closes, users are more likely to make use of mediation, using it to replace the current default of arbitration. Growing demand would in turn allow states to respond by ratifying the Singapore Convention. The next section outlines a possible way to expand the scope of mediation, by using arbitration.

B. *Using arbitration to further mediation*

Parties can utilise mediation within the arbitration framework by drafting their dispute resolution clause in a way that gives effect to this intention. Multi-tiered dispute resolution clauses are gaining popularity for their "best of all worlds" prospect. In fact, greater institutional support for such clauses is now being seen, especially as prominent arbitral institutions including the Singapore International Arbitration Centre ("**SIAC**"), International Court of Arbitration ("**ICC**") or London Court of International Arbitration ("**LCIA**") provide for model tiered dispute resolution clauses. This highlights the building of a harmonious ecosystem for the international dispute resolution regime.

One particularly useful collaboration between SIAC and Singapore International Mediation Centre ("**SIMC**") is the Arb-Med-Arb protocol. The protocol, which was introduced prior to the coming into effect of the Singapore Convention, allows parties that have commenced arbitration to stay the arbitral proceedings as the dispute is referred to mediation under the aegis of SIMC. If the dispute is resolved, the settlement agreement is passed as an arbitral award under the SIAC instituted arbitration. Further, while the dispute is pending in mediation, the arbitration is kept on hold.

Since its introduction, the protocol has been enthusiastically promoted by both SIAC and SIMC, as well as the Singapore Government. An important reason for this protocol to be preferred over med-arb processes is because it addresses any doubts on enforcement resulting from an arbitration (in med-arb) not being instituted for a live dispute.[17]

It is suggested that the Arb-Med-Arb protocol was first introduced to give effect to mediated settlement agreements.[18] However, this process is not without its criticisms, which includes ambiguity as to interim measures. How are interim measures to be ordered by the tribunal if the dispute is stayed immediately due to mediation? The other ambiguous part of the protocol is with regard to the raising of jurisdictional objections. When can parties raise jurisdictional objections to the tribunal? [19]

Another shortcoming of this process is that it results in parties incurring more costs than they would if they had simply referred their dispute to mediation. When the Singapore Convention gains greater acceptance, perhaps the need for this protocol may vanish. However, until that happens, it is suggested that this protocol or other such innovative measures that allow parties to make use of mediation must be encouraged. This will result in an increased familiarisation with the process of mediation, which in turn promises to lead to a growth of mediation.

V. Conclusion

The above discussion highlights how the Singapore Convention came into existence to fill a void that existed to give effect to settlement agreements. Together with the New York Convention, it gives international private law two strong conventions, as opposed to one. These are, after all, two pieces in the puzzle of international dispute resolution. The success of the Singapore Convention rests on the combined willingness of states, practitioners and users to give effect to the Convention.

One suggestion is that at a national level, states must keep ahead of the parties to support the growth of mediation by ratifying the Singapore Convention and contributing to its growth. When one country ratifies the Singapore Convention, other countries that typically trade with that country will be more likely to ratify the Convention as well.

At the same time, it is a duty of the lawyers representing parties to help them to make use of mediation when this mode of dispute resolution is more suited for their case. For example, practitioners can encourage parties to make use of multi-tiered dispute resolution clauses, such as the Arb-Med-Arb protocol, if it is more appropriate for their situation.

Even though this objective of popularising the Singapore Convention is not yet achieved, mediation should not be parked aside. It should be embraced using the existing models that currently enjoy a stronghold over the dispute resolution space.

https://doi.org/10.1142/9789819825042_0007

Chapter 7

Safeguards or Overregulation? A Dive into Mediator Standards Under the Singapore Convention

Mervyn Lin Zheng Hong

I. Introduction

The United Nations Convention on International Settlement Agreements resulting from Mediation ("**the Singapore Convention**")[1] serves as an important piece of legislation, helping to burnish the reputation of mediation by increasing its attractiveness as a form of dispute resolution for international commercial disputes. It addresses the issues of cross-jurisdictional enforcement of settlement agreements by creating a way for parties to enforce their mediation agreements across jurisdictions. However, in doing so, it raises several important questions.

A particular provision which has been the subject of discussion amongst academics is the inclusion of Article 5(1)(e) of the Singapore Convention. Article 5 of the Singapore Convention provides several grounds for refusal to grant relief where relief is sought under Article 4 of the Singapore Convention. Article 5(1)(e) of the Singapore Convention specifically allows for the refusal to grant relief where "there was a serious breach by the mediator of standards applicable to the mediator or the mediation without which breach that party would not have entered into the settlement agreement."

The provision imposes legal obligations onto mediators by codifying the idea of mediation standards. This essay will analyse whether the legal weight imposed on mediation standards is a beneficial development in the field of mediation, and if so, what standards should be read into the provision.

II. The Idea of Mediator Standards

The Case for Mediator Standards

Firstly, in order to understand the utility of Article 5(1)(e) of the Singapore Convention, we must analyse if we should endeavour to even consider the idea of mediation standards. Are standards useful in guiding mediators or are they hindrances to the process?

A) *Legitimacy*

The idea of mediation standards is useful insofar as they guarantee a certain level of legitimacy in the process. Traditionally, one of the reasons why mediation has been perceived as a weaker form of dispute resolution is the uncertainty of its outcome. Parties can agree to mediate and spend hours on discussions, but may end up leaving without reaching a settlement agreement.

This is because ultimately, mediators do not impose decisions and it is the parties who have to decide to come to an agreement. This can create ambiguity for the parties with regard to how the mediator adds value to the resolution of the dispute, which in turn generally results in reduced confidence in the mediation process.

By establishing a set of standards which mediators must abide by, parties can be assured of a certain level of proficiency and value from the mediator. For example, should there be a certain guarantee of impartiality and interest-mining by all mediators, parties who feel that they have not been heard in court would find confidence in attempting the mediation process. This is because it would at least guarantee them the opportunity to voice their concerns.

B) *Protection*

Further, they would also be given some sort of recourse should the mediator not meet these minimum standards, especially in situations in which standards fall exceptionally short. For example, in the case of ***Vitakis Valchine v Valchine***,[2] one party alleged that the mediator had employed significant coercion and duress to get her to sign the mediated settlement agreement. In view of such cases and the increasing popularity of mediation, experts have stressed the need for greater protection for mediating parties.[3] An example of this would be refusing relief under the aforementioned Article 5 of the Singapore Convention.

The Case Against Mediator Standards

However, there are also significant principal arguments against the concept of mediation standards.

A) *Compromise on key tenets of flexibility and party autonomy*

Firstly, imposing standards may infringe on the process of mediation. Mediation is a process that is inherently flexible and dynamic and hence, it would be extremely difficult to quantify a set of applicable standards without compromising these factors. This is because it would be difficult to establish exactly what mediators ought to do during a mediation as this could vary widely depending on the facts of each case.

This is notably different from other forms of dispute resolution, such as arbitration or litigation, where arbitrators or judges play a determinative role in the outcome.[4] For example, in arbitration, protections for parties against illegitimate arbitrators focus on assessing the legitimacy of the arbitral award. This could be through analysing whether the arbitrator exceeded their jurisdiction.[5] This is because generally, the standard of the arbitration can be ascertained through the award given and the reasoning behind the imposition of the award.

By contrast, this is not the case for mediation as the mediator is not the one who determines the final settlement. Additionally, due to its flexible nature, it is difficult to pinpoint exactly which part of the mediation process that mediator standards should be imposed upon. The imposition of an overly stringent set of standards may compromise important core benefits of mediation — that of flexibility and adaptability.

Nevertheless, it is submitted that not all applicable standards would unduly restrict the process of mediation, but rather only those that are too onerous. It is still possible to impose minimum standards upon mediators in order to guarantee a certain level of proficiency whilst not hindering the mediation process itself. In fact, mediator standards, if crafted correctly, can further protect certain core values in the process. The question which will be tackled in the next section then is what standards should be applied and particularly in this case, what standards Article 5(1)(e) of the Singapore Convention should be referring to.

B) *Mediator's lack of culpability*

Any issues concerning the enforcement of the settlement should not involve the mediator, due to the emphasis on self-determination of the parties. Rather issues with enforcement should be directed at those involved in making the decision to enter into the settlement agreement, namely the parties and their legal counsel.[6]

In most commercial disputes, parties are likely to be represented by counsel who are tasked with representing and protecting the client's interests during the mediation.[7] In such mediations, it could be argued that counsel should shoulder greater culpability should an illegitimate or disadvantageous agreement be reached. This is because mediators are there only to facilitate the process, while counsel are specifically tasked to protect their clients.

Hence, causes of action by parties should be directed towards their counsel instead, through avenues available to them in tort or contract law. Notably, this means that even if they cannot take action against a mediator because of the removal of mediator standards, parties will still have legal recourse against their counsel.

However, this argument only holds weight if counsel shoulders full responsibility for the outcome of the settlement. This proposition does not reflect the realities of modern mediation. There is an abundance of literature to suggest that mediators hold a certain power over the process, through their position as third parties, and would be able to affect the eventual settlement agreement.

The mediator's contribution to the agreement reached has also received widespread recognition in numerous legal documents. In fact, Article 2(3) of the Singapore Convention defines mediation as a process through which parties attempt to reach a settlement of their dispute harmoniously with the assistance of mediators. Additionally, if mediators really lack an ability to impact the settlement agreement, no one would be engaging in mediation at all. Hence, while mediators are not able to issue judgements, they still contribute significantly to any resolution arrived at through mediation. As such, they should still be held accountable for their actions through the establishment of mediation standards.

In conclusion, while there are several principal issues surrounding the idea of imposing mediation standards, the practical benefits cannot be overlooked. Further, many of the issues created by the improper application of standards can be mitigated through the deliberate and careful application of standards. That said, as this paper will tackle below, crafting appropriate and effective standards for mediation is a complex endeavour.

III. Applicable Mediator Standards

The question now turns to what "applicable standards" ought best to apply to mediators under the Singapore Convention.

There are several schools of thought on this issue. Generally, the Singapore Convention seems to suggest that each mediation should be judged by its own standards, either by agreement between parties and the mediator, or prescribed by the code of conduct of the mediator's organisation. This paper will examine the benefits and limitations of such a reading and consider several suggestions as to how the provision can be improved.

Flexible Standards as the Status Quo

The reading of the term "standards" seems to align with the drafters of the Singapore Convention. In the *travaux preparatoires,* specific reference was made by the working group to the "the law governing conciliation and codes of conduct, including those developed by professional associations" when reference was made to "applicable standards".[8] Generally, in practice, this means that mediators will be bound by the standards or codes of conduct applicable to their accreditation institution or standards agreed to between the parties. This means that every mediation will be bound by different standards.

A) *Benefits*

The benefits of such flexible standards are clear. Firstly, they provide for greater party autonomy over the process. In line with the core tenets of voluntariness and party self-determination, parties ought to be empowered to shape the mediation process according to their needs. For example, if parties want the mediator to be more involved, they can choose a set of standards that would allow the mediator to take a more participative role, one that lies closer to the evaluative mediation model. This could give the mediator greater freedom to suggest options. Conversely, if parties want greater self-determination, they can opt for standards that focus on the mediator's role as a facilitator.

Secondly, it retains mediator flexibility. Similar to how parties benefit from increased autonomy, mediators are better able to adapt how they approach mediation on a case-by-case basis. Should the mediator feel that they ought to intervene more in the discussion, they can ask for the parties' consent and proceed to adjust the way they approach the mediation process. This is not something that would be possible with a rigid set of uniform standards.

Finally, barring alteration by the parties, the mediator's familiarity with their accreditation institution's standards would allow for greater efficiency in mediation. Currently, different mediation institutes impose different mediation standards on their mediators. Allowing mediators to work within the boundaries they were trained and accredited in would allow them to handle the mediation in the most efficient way.

Imposing greater restrictions on mediators who were trained under more flexible standards may prove challenging. For example, while the Singapore Mediation Centre's ("**SMC**") Mediators Code of Conduct does bring up the importance of impartiality, it generally leaves it to the discretion of the mediator as to how this would be specifically carried out during the mediation.

This contrasts with the Singapore International Mediation Institute's ("**SIMI**") Code of Professional Conduct ("**CPC**") for SIMI Mediators, which provides for more specific requirements with regard to the concept of impartiality. This can be seen in Article 5 of the SIMI's CPC which breaks down the specific steps the mediator should take to ensure impartiality, such as enforcing equal opportunity of private communication under Article 5.6 of the SIMI's CPC or the greater restrictions that apply when the mediator wants to draw on personal expertise under Article 5.10 of the SIMI's CPC.

An SMC trained mediator would thus find it restrictive when approaching mediation under SIMI's Code. This is not to say that one set of standards is more desirable than the other, but rather to illustrate that standards can differ substantially across institutions. Hence, greater flexibility in applicable standards is beneficial for mediators as they will have the ability to work under the standards they were trained in.

B) *Potential issues*

However, there are several issues with this flexible application of mediation standards. Firstly, the process of designating standards may be difficult to enforce in practice. This will include instances where parties and the mediator do not decide on applicable standards applied in the mediation. The *Harvard Negotiation Law Review* published a study that showed the results of Fran Tetunic's investigation of hundreds of mediator contracts. He found that provisions creating mediators' responsibilities were absent from most of the contracts and this consequently made it difficult to define a mediator's obligations.[9]

The absence of designated standards leads to issues where it would be difficult to determine which standards of mediation ought to apply. The competent authority would have to resort to a relatively uncertain process of determination by looking at the facts of the case. If no standards can be determined, it has been suggested that the party's defence cannot be supported based on Article 5(1)(e) of the Singapore Convention.

Moreover, this may be problematic for parties unfamiliar with mediation (like those from jurisdictions where mediation has only been recently adopted), and they would be severely disadvantaged. Given that the Singapore Convention aims to encourage companies to begin using mediation, it is likely that many parties to mediation inspired by this Convention may be attempting the process for the first time.

Further, in places where mediators may not be as regulated, this also creates a disincentive for mediators to be upfront about the inclusion of such standards. Ironically, this creates the situation where the very group of people Article 5(1)(e) of the Singapore Convention aims to target — problematic mediators — would be the ones best able to avoid it.

Another potential issue would be the lack of commercial certainty. With different individual standards applicable to individual mediations, parties who attempt multiple mediations may find themselves subject to different standards. This uncertainty may foster greater hesitation in considering mediation as a dispute resolution mechanism.[10]

Notably, this uncertainty creates issues when parties hope to include dispute resolution clauses within their agreements. Parties are unable to foresee how mediations will be conducted and may find it too pre-emptive to include mediation as a dispute resolution mechanism. As such many parties may be disincentivised to consider mediation as a reliable option to resolve disputes. This runs counter to what the Singapore Convention hopes to achieve, which is the promotion of mediation.

IV. Possible Refinements to "Standards" Under Article 5(1)(e) of the Singapore Convention

A. *The creation of a unified standard of mediation*

This view suggests that the implementation of Article 5(1)(e) of the Singapore Convention would benefit from having an accompanying unified standard of mediators, applicable to all mediations. This would benefit the provision as it addresses issues of uncertainty within the provision.

The main concern with such unified standards would be determining what standards to apply across diverse jurisdictions. It is well understood that while mediation as a process has been adopted internationally, the manner in which mediation is conducted can vary substantially. Expectations of mediations can vary due to the differences in cultures between jurisdictions.[11]

To illustrate this, one can take reference to Hofstede's cultural dimensions model.[12] The model has been used to represent such cultural differences and through this we can better understand how these differences may affect the mediation process. For example, China and the United States of America ("**USA**") have different Power Distance Index values, with

China scoring high while the USA scores low. This means that parties from China are likely to be more stringent with regards to authority and hierarchy whereas parties from the USA are likely to lean towards shared authority and flat organisational structures. Applying this to mediations, parties in Chinese mediations may expect mediators to refrain from involving themselves in shifting power dynamics between parties. Conversely, parties in American mediation may expect the opposite, expecting the mediator to act as a conduit to balance power imbalances.

Hence, when it comes to determining a single set of standards, it would be difficult to prioritise the practices of one jurisdiction over another. Any effort to do so may result in standards that do not accurately reflect the practices of mediation in a particular jurisdiction. This potentially alienates entire mediation communities.

However, it has been suggested that a unified standard need not be so specific but rather serve as a principled guide for which additional standards could apply. A set of core principles was discussed by the working group during the conception of the Singapore Convention. Notably the elements of independence, impartiality, fair treatment and confidentiality are potential foundation values for mediation. This would act as a compromise between over-regulation of the mediation process at one end of the spectrum, and a complete lack of oversight at the other. This would also guarantee the protection of certain core tenets of mediation generally accepted across jurisdictions but also leave room for parties and mediators to develop other mediation principles that they deem necessary.

Thus, while a certain level of unified standards could address the present issues with Article 5(1)(e) of the Singapore Convention, it is important to consider the extent to which these standards could affect current practices of mediation.

B. *Code of disclosure*

Another approach that has been discussed is the idea of a unified Code of Disclosure.[13] This code would impose the obligation on the mediator to disclose a standardised set of information about the mediation. This would include relevant information such as the applicable standards governing the mediator's conduct, steps in the mediation process and style of mediation, amongst others. For example, the SIMI's CPC already provides for this under Articles 3 and 5. This, importantly, supports the parties' right to self-determination whilst protecting the tenet of flexibility in the process.

However, it should be noted that disclosure alone does not guarantee that the mediator will perform to set standards. If parties are completely unaware of standard mediation practices, they may still be susceptible to unknowingly relinquishing their rights and procedural safeguards. Nevertheless, it is submitted that under this code, the risk is significantly reduced and parties would clearly be informed of the relevant information.

V. Conclusion

The discussion of mediation standards is not a novel one. Countries and institutions that support mediation often grapple with this issue as they strive to encourage growth in the industry. However, the Singapore Convention is novel in that it was created to support the development of mediation in a global landscape. In doing so, it is presented with new issues, exacerbated by the Convention's international nature.

In conclusion, it is submitted that the current interpretation of standards of mediation under Article 5(1)(e) of the Singapore Convention is too broad and uncertain to effectively achieve what the provision sets out to do. In line with several of the papers cited in this paper, refinements are needed to fully realise the potential of the Singapore Convention. Nevertheless, the issue on mediation standards is one that is ever changing. Even as mediation itself evolves over time, drafters and authorities can also keep in mind the inherent flexibility and evolution of the mediation process and not be afraid to tackle new issues as they surface.

https://doi.org/10.1142/9789819825042_0008

Chapter 8

Should Third-Party Funding Be Extended to Stand-Alone Mediation?

Neo Win Kyi

I. Introduction

Third-party funding ("**TPF**") refers to the funding of legal proceedings by an entity unconnected to a dispute in return for financial gain, such as a share of awarded damages or the settlement sum.[1] The Civil Law (Amendment) Act 2017 validates third-party funding contracts, which set out the rights and obligations of both the funder and the funded party.

TPF is distinct from but may be combined with other forms of financial dispute resolution permitted in Singapore, such as lawyer contingency fees, pro bono legal services, litigation loans, and various forms of insurance.[2] However, this essay specifically focusses on financing that is motivated by direct financial interest in the outcome of the dispute, excluding financing that is regulated through other legal regimes.

Traditionally, TPF agreements for dispute resolution are prohibited under the common law doctrines of maintenance and champerty. In Singapore, such prohibitions also manifest in the law of contract, which renders agreements void if affected by maintenance and champerty for being contrary to public policy.[3] Many jurisdictions forbid TPF to protect vulnerable individuals from being oppressed by wealthy funders, to avoid unwarranted interferences with the process of justice, as well as to prevent excessive and frivolous claims.[4,5]

However, the presence of other safeguards against fraud and abuse in legal systems today challenges the importance of the prohibition. Furthermore, the high cost of dispute resolution has increased business demand for financing options for dispute resolution.

These developments have led many jurisdictions to abolish the tort of maintenance and champerty, leading to a rise in TPF in dispute resolution. Singapore has followed suit, with Parliament passing the Civil Law (Amendment) Act 2017, abolishing the common law tort of maintenance and champerty and permitting TPF for international arbitration proceedings and related court and mediation proceedings.[4] The scope of the law was later expanded in 2021 to include domestic arbitration proceedings and related court proceedings, proceedings in the Singapore International Commercial Court ("**SICC**"), appeal proceedings arising from SICC decisions, and related mediation proceedings.[6]

Despite the rising popularity of TPF and local efforts to promote mediation as a method of dispute resolution,[7] TPF is still not permitted for stand-alone mediation. As mentioned, mediation funding is limited to cases arising from arbitral proceedings, such as Med-Arb or Arb-Med-Arb, or SICC proceedings — though Senior Minister of State for Law Indranee Rajah SC hinted that this may change in the future.[8]

Hence, this essay discusses whether TPF should be extended to all mediation proceedings in Singapore, as is now the case in Hong Kong. This essay will first assess the effect of extending TPF to mediation, given the principles of mediation. Next, this essay will cover existing issues in TPF and their implications on TPF mediation. Finally, this essay will examine the impact of TPF on public policy. My conclusion is that the extension of TPF to stand-alone mediation is currently unnecessary.

II. Effect of Extending TPF to Mediation (Given the Principles of Mediation)

A. *Flow of proceedings is affected by the compromise on confidentiality in mediation under TPF*

Discussions and information shared during mediation are confidential. Under section 9(1) of the Mediation Act 2017, a person must not disclose any mediation communication relating to a mediation to any external third party. Mediation communication refers to anything said or done, any document prepared, or any information provided during the mediation process or for its purposes. This includes the mediation agreement or mediated settlement agreement. Confidentiality is important as it encourages parties to freely discuss interests and explore solutions without fear that the information will be used against them outside of the mediation process.

The introduction of TPF risks undermining this confidentiality, and may consequently affect parties' willingness to engage in the process of mediation. The disclosure of mediation communication to third-party funders, which may be requested by the funder, is allowed under section 9(2) of the Mediation Act if the consent of all parties to the mediation is given.

Furthermore, third-party funders may be present at mediation proceedings. Their presence may compromise the funded party's willingness to share their interests or concerns transparently during the mediation, for fear that the funder will use the information shared against the funded party, particularly if the mediation settlement is not reached or money awarded is not satisfactory to the funder. Such dynamics affect the flow of discussions and the prospect of reaching a settlement agreement.

Funded parties in third-party funded arbitrations or SICC proceedings share the same concern. Although matters relating to the proceeding may be kept confidential from the public, a funder's knowledge of what goes on during the proceedings may be used against the funded party.[9–11]

The issue of confidentiality is especially significant in mediation, where confidentiality affects the flow of the proceeding itself. Professor Elayne Greenberg posits that the purpose of confidentiality in mediation differs from that in other types of proceedings. It allows parties to the mediation to share their interests freely and "collaborate to develop a party-directed resolution".[12,13] While conflict discourse in arbitration and litigation is bound by the procedural rules of evidence or discovery, parties to mediation are free to "engage in conflict conversations that are candid rather than positional rants".[14,15] This candour, fostered by strict confidentiality, is central to facilitating understanding and collaborative problem solving needed to achieve meaningful, party-directed settlements.[16–18] When confidentiality of mediation is compromised by the involvement of third-party funders, the effectiveness of mediation proceedings can be severely affected.

B. *Settlement under the principle of self-determination in mediation is hindered by TPF*

Unlike arbitration, where the decision-making power lies in the arbitrator, mediation allows parties to make their own decisions to resolve their dispute. However, the introduction of TPF easily influences parties' decisions, altering the dynamics of mediation and hindering settlement. This is illustrated in the article "How Third-Party Funders Change the Chemistry of Settlements" by Barbara Reeves, who draws from her experience as a mediator and arbitrator to show how funding affects party behaviour.

Reeves posits that each party comes to mediation with two reference points. The first is their aspirational settlement, which are the ideal terms they each hope the case will settle at, and the second is their bottom-line settlement, which are the minimum terms they are willing to accept if they have to. When parties choose between a certain settlement outcome and an uncertain trial outcome, they evaluate options as either gains or losses relative to those reference points.[19]

The introduction of a third-party funder shifts parties' reference points in several ways, changing their evaluation of whether an option is seen as a gain or a loss, which can disrupt settlement. There are three reasons why this happens.

Firstly, a third-party funder's investment in a case creates an endorsement effect on the funded party's case, affecting the funded party's reference points.[20] If the settlement reference points overlap with that of the other party, a bargaining range is produced and a settlement can be reached.[21] However, if the funded party "substantially overestimates" its chance of success in the mediation or future proceedings because of the endorsement effect, the bargaining range is likely to narrow or disappear, inhibiting settlement.[22]

Secondly, as the funder is entitled to a portion of the settlement proceeds, the funded party must deduct both legal fees and the funder's share when evaluating any offer.[23] This raises the funded party's reference points, which may cause the funded party to view a certain offer as a loss rather than a gain because of the amount owed to the funder.

Thirdly, a funder's reference points may influence the funded party's initial reference points. Given that there is likely a disparity between a funder and funded party's net worth, they would view the same settlement offer differently — relative to their individual net worth.[24] A funder has sunk costs and expectations. To maximise returns, a funder will try to persuade the funded party that a case is worth more than the funded party's initial reference points. Hence, an offer which was initially viewed as a gain may now be construed as a loss by the funded party, discouraging its acceptance and impeding settlement.[25] Furthermore, if a settlement offer is less than what the funder anticipates, the funder may even choose to advance the mediation to other forms of dispute resolution like trial proceedings.

Lastly, a funder may level the playing field with regard to the parties' relative resources.[26] This signals to the non-funded party that a war of attrition will not work as the funded party has greater staying power, causing the non-funded party to raise its reference points for settlement.[27] This poses the question of whether any increase in the non-funded party's reference points will be sufficient to increase the bargaining range in light of the funded party's reference points which have also increased due to the aforementioned effects.[28]

Not only can funders influence the power dynamics between parties, strategy of negotiations and substance of a settlement, but some funding agreements may also grant funders the right to veto a settlement that the parties would have otherwise agreed on. Since funders are not subjected to professional conduct rules or fiduciary duties to funded parties, funders' interests may not align with that of the funded parties, distorting the dynamics of settlement discussions.[29]

The extent to which a funder can participate in settlement discussions is determined by domestic laws for funding contracts and funded proceedings, thereby highlighting its importance in upholding the independence of parties and integrity of proceedings. Funding contracts may give funders the right of approval of the settlement, or provide how a dispute will be settled if a funder and funded party do not agree, such as appointing a senior counsel to act as a "tie-breaker".[30] Though to a smaller extent, third-party funded arbitration is also affected by the participation of third-party funders in key strategic decisions.[31,32]

Empirical evidence suggests that disclosing the existence of a funding arrangement to the mediator may aid parties in reaching a settlement. Such transparency may allow the mediator to assess the impact of TPF on what appears to be a rational bargaining range, and hence factor that impact into settlement negotiations.[33]

The value of disclosure of TPF is recognised in Rule 49A of the Legal Profession (Professional Conduct) Rules 2015, which requires a legal practitioner to disclose the existence of any funding contract and the identity of the funder to the court or tribunal and every other party to the dispute resolution proceeding.[34] This rule not only promotes transparency in proceedings, but also prevents conflicts of interest that may occur between the arbitrator or mediator, funder, funded party or legal counsel.

C. *The attractiveness of mediation funding is affected by the non-adversarial nature and resolution uncertainty of mediation*

Mediation is meant to be non-adversarial and focused on collaborative problem-solving, placing an emphasis on preserving relationships and achieving mutually beneficial outcomes. This sets mediation apart from other dispute resolution methods like arbitration, which is characterised by a position-based approach.[35]

TPF of mediation hence poses a few issues. Firstly, there is the question of how the doctrines of maintenance and champerty would apply to mediation.[36] Secondly, the collaborative ethos of mediation makes it unattractive to funders. Funders typically prioritise getting higher returns from higher settlement sums. If a funder pressures the parties to settle for a higher amount to secure a return on investment, it compromises the non-adversarial nature of mediation. However, if the funder does not interfere in the mediation to push for a higher settlement amount, the outcome may not be financially worthwhile, making the investment unprofitable. Hence, finding a funder for mediation would be difficult.

The fact that mediation does not impose a decision on parties makes mediation even more unattractive to fund. While arbitration and litigation provide binding decisions enforceable in court, mediation outcomes are only binding if parties enter into a settlement agreement. Such agreements are typically enforceable as contracts under Singapore law. However, additional enforcement mechanisms exist; parties may apply to have the agreement recorded as a court order under the Mediation Act 2017, or if the dispute is international and commercial in nature, seek cross-border enforcement under the Singapore Convention on Mediation.

If no settlement is reached, a decision will not be imposed on the parties. Failure of the mediation process is essentially a "financial stalemate", whereby both parties incur the cost of their unresolved dispute.[37] While mediation is often more cost-effective compared to litigation or arbitration, funders are deterred by the uncertainty of recovery, particularly with regard to whether they can collect the award or recoup legal costs from the other party in mediation.[38]

Given the uncertainty on the success of reaching a resolution in mediation, it is often followed by or used in conjunction with other dispute resolution methods like litigation or arbitration. This is illustrated by multi-stage dispute resolution processes like Med-Arb, Arb-Med-Arb and SICC's Lit-Med-Lit regime, which are more likely to attract funders. Lawyer Anthanasios Papadas posits that the combination of mediation with other forms of dispute resolution methods is the reason the convergence of TPF with mediation has not been discussed as extensively as that of other dispute resolution methods.[39] Under the current structure, pure mediation is simply "not economically viable" for profit-driven funders.[40]

III. Existing Issues in TPF which Further Hinder its Extension to Stand-Alone Mediation

A. *Disclosure of information to funders*

As funders' returns depend on the success of the proceedings, especially the amount of any award rendered and the enforcement risk, funders will usually conduct thorough due diligence by seeking extensive information on the proceedings from the funded party.[41] While non-disclosure agreements may be used to preserve confidentiality, the fear of waiver of privilege may affect the funded party's involvement in proceedings as the funded party may view such disclosure of information to the funder as a weakness in the proceedings. The funded party may compensate for this by being less transparent in mediation proceedings, affecting the reaching of a settlement where understanding is key. The concern of sharing information with a funder is also prevalent in third party-funded arbitrations, especially for disclosure requests in arbitral proceedings.[42]

B. *Difficulties and costs in obtaining funding*

As mentioned, whether a proceeding is funded depends on a funder's assessment of the predicted returns and enforcement risk of a case.[43]

Given the need to provide attractive returns to investors, funders are highly selective in choosing the claims they fund, with fewer than 1 in 30 applications assessed being funded.[44] Given the relatively low profitability and uncertainty of mediation proceedings to funders, one may doubt whether funders will ever consider funding stand-alone mediations.

Even if one acquires TPF, financial support comes at a significant cost. Funders usually contract for a substantial portion of an award, often between 20 to 40 per cent of the compensation awarded.[45,46] This means that even if the funded party is successful in their claim, they will only receive a fraction of the awarded amount after deducting funding, legal and procedural costs, which may not always be recoverable from the other party.[47]

Funded parties may need to apply for security of costs to enforce a costs order against the other party, either domestically or internationally. Such applications entail further costs and may be wasted if the application is unsuccessful as these applications are highly subjective based on jurisdiction and arbitral rules.[48–51] While the SICC Procedural Guide provides some guidance on these applications, outcomes remain uncertain and context-dependent. Such great efforts for small rewards raise the question of whether it is worth pursuing TPF, especially for proceedings with uncertain outcomes like mediation. This hence challenges the necessity of extending TPF to stand-alone mediation.

IV. The Impact of TPF on Public Policy

A. *Potential abuses of TPF*

Mediation plays a pivotal role in settling personal injury claims. As opposed to arbitration or SICC proceedings, mediation often involves individual claimants rather than commercial parties. Many of these individuals are vulnerable and may lack legal acumen or financial resources. Without a legislative carve-out for personal injury mediation, the expansion of TPF to stand-alone mediation could embolden touts and recovery agents to profit from such cases.[52]

B. *Increase in marginal claims which may shape the law*

Despite funders' detailed assessment of the merits of the claims they fund, the expansion of TPF may increase the pursuit of marginal cases, which have the potential to shape the legal landscape in a more claimant- and funder-friendly direction.[53]

V. Evaluation

Mediation is a unique dispute resolution method, with specific principles that guide its proceedings, such as confidentiality and party self-determination. Such principles may be compromised by TPF or allow funders to hinder settlement. Furthermore, the non-adversarial nature and resolution uncertainty in mediation diminishes a funder's chances of earning big returns, making stand-alone mediation a less attractive vehicle for profit-driven funders.

One's choice to seek TPF as a financing option is also affected by existing issues in the current framework. Taken together, these factors impact the demand and supply of TPF for mediation and question the need to spend time and money extending the TPF framework to stand-alone mediation, rendering extension impractical.

Establishing a comprehensive regulatory framework is not straightforward in the context of pre-existing procedural rules applicable to different dispute resolution proceedings, court and legal counsel, national laws and regulations, investment treaties and relevant conventions. Extending the TPF framework will also likely increase the number and complexity of claims raised, thus increasing the price of regulation.[54] While the Law Society of Singapore has issued Guidance Note 10.1.1 on TPF, Singapore will need to contextualise this to the specifics of mediation like Hong Kong's Code of Practice for Third Party Funding of Mediation.

Even if the perceived benefits of extending the TPF framework outweigh the risks, policymakers in Singapore would need to consider the impact of legal reforms promoting TPF on public policy. The regulation of TPF is "relatively recent" and is "intended to balance the benefits of increased access to justice with safeguards against potential abuses".[55]

Extending TPF to stand-alone mediation necessitates significant regulatory adjustments to ensure that such funding operates within the same standards of accountability and ethical considerations as they do in arbitration and litigation.[56] While such considerations should not deter efforts in expanding the framework, it does call for a more careful and gradual expansion to minimise adverse effects of TPF on public policy.

Ultimately, the law surrounding mediation will strengthen as the dispute resolution develops amidst trends like TPF, as long as intentional effort is expended in balancing parties' considerations with the country's policy considerations.

https://doi.org/10.1142/9789819825042_0009

Chapter 9

Cultural Dynamics in International Mediation: Anthropological Insights for Effective Conflict Resolution

Ng Hui En, Helene

I. Introduction

In the early decades of the 21st century, the spectre of global conflict looms, casting a shadow over the delicate fabric of international relations. In this era of interconnectedness, the stakes of diplomacy have never been higher. Against this backdrop of strife, mediation emerges as a beacon of hope in our increasingly fractured world. This essay examines the intersection of anthropology and mediation tactics in international relations and explores how an anthropological perspective can make mediation outcomes more culturally effective and equitable for conflicting cultures.

Drawing upon anthropology can infuse international relations mediation with insights into culture and behaviour, and make it a transformative practice with the potential to defuse tensions and foster peace through common ground brought about by increased awareness of complex cultural dynamics at play.

II. Mediation Framework and Definition

Mediation involves a third party who facilitates the reduction of differences or seeks a solution during a conflict.[1] In intercultural international relations mediation, people often perceive themselves and others through the lens of their social, cultural, and ethnic identities.

According to Huntington's Clash of Civilisations theory, "In the post-Cold War world, the most important distinctions among peoples are cultural." While his propositions are often criticised, it is true that the success of mediation frequently depends on the parties' ability to understand and respect each other's culturally defined interests, for significant cultural differences can intensify conflicts and make resolution more challenging. Empirical evidence has shown that the more prominent cultural issues are in a dispute, the harder it is to resolve it amicably. International relations mediators must thus recognise and validate cultural differences and distinct identities to foster trust and facilitate constructive dialogue.[2]

Anthropological perspectives thus highlight the importance of identity affirmation in mediation processes to address underlying tensions and promote reconciliation.[3] Abramson suggested a four-step approach for cross-culture mediators: (1) understanding their own culture, (2) researching the other party's culture, (3) bridging any cultural gap, and (4) considering withdrawal when necessary due to irreconcilable values.[4]

Gellman, reflecting on her mediation experience during the Cambodian crisis, effectively illustrates this approach. She reflects on how her low-context, individualistic background from the United States made it challenging for her to mediate in the high-context Cambodian environment, where implicit communication and the collective good were prioritised. Effective international relations mediators thus need to be aware of their cultural differences and consciously shift their communication patterns in order to connect effectively with those from other cultures.[5]

III. How Anthropology Can Create Culturally Sensitive Mediation Outcomes

Anthropology is the broad study of human culture and development, and spans fields ranging from history to evolutionary biology.[6] Assuming these factors are the underlying force behind conflicts, mediating international disputes with pre-existing complex cultural dynamics means that mediators have to confront the twin dangers of cultural imperialism and cultural relativism.

A. *Cultural imperialism*

Cultural imperialism refers to the imposition of one culture's values, beliefs, and norms on another, often resulting in the marginalisation or erasure of the latter's cultural identity. Western paradigms, which dominate international relations mediation, often show cultural imperialism, as they frequently overlook indigenous norms and practices.[7]

A key example of how imposing Western frameworks on non-Western cultural contexts can lead to ineffective mediation outcomes is the Dayton Accords. It was negotiated in 1995 and led by the United States to achieve peace amidst the Bosnian war. The Dayton Accords were heavily influenced by Western norms of governance, and failed to consider the deeply rooted cultural and communal aspects of the conflict. Bosnia and Herzegovina have a long history of ethnic diversity, with significant populations of Bosniaks, Serbs, and Croats. This historical fragmentation was not addressed by the Dayton Accords, and a Western style of negotiation that prioritised state-centric solutions over community reconciliation and local customs was proposed.[8]

Instead of reconciliation and ethnic harmony, the agreement created a highly complex divisive political structure, dividing Bosnia and Herzegovina into two entities with a strong central government. In Annex 4 of the peace accords, the Parliamentary Assembly structure institutionalised ethnic divisions by requiring representation based on ethnic identity, enforcing ethnic lines rather than a unified national identity.[9] Political positions at all levels of government in Bosnia and Herzegovina are allocated based on affiliation to only Bosniaks, Serbs, or Croats. If individuals identify with any other ethnicity, they are legally excluded from attaining political leadership positions in the country, perpetuating ethnic inequality.[10]

Although the Dayton Accords successfully halted the war in the short run with its focus on military and political action, it has been criticised for entrenching ethnic divisions rather than promoting a multi-ethnic society, due to its lack of anthropological consideration for the diverse ethnic groups of the country.

This illuminates how the inherently Western approach to international relations struggles to handle cultural differences, repeating the same patterns of thought, and mirroring colonialism. International relations adversely impact mediation by ignoring or misunderstanding the perspectives of non-Western cultures, failing to address unique contexts moulding conflicts and causing ineffective or biased mediation outcomes. By utilising ethnography, allowing for a deeper understanding of diverse cultures and histories, international relations mediation can become more inclusive and effective.[11]

B. *Cultural relativism*

Cultural relativism can lead to the uncritical acceptance of harmful practices. While cultural relativism encourages respect for diverse cultural perspectives, it posits that all cultural practices and beliefs are equally valid within their own context, and external judgments should be suspended.[12] Such relativism may lead to reluctance or inability to critique actions perpetuating violence or injustice, due to the assumption that they are inherent to the cultures involved.

This inability to critique actions perpetuating the violation of human rights can be seen in a case study in Myanmar. An Independent International Fact-Finding Mission on Myanmar was established by the United Nations ("**UN**") Human Rights Council in 2017 to look into the claims of human rights violations perpetrated by Myanmar against the Rohingya. Under Myanmar's 1982 Citizenship Law, the Rohingya are denied citizenship, leaving them stateless. This is also an indirect means of justifying the 2017 atrocities against them, as the Myanmar government can deny responsibility with regard to the Rohingya human rights abuse due to their statelessness. Despite official UN resolutions denouncing the abuses, cultural relativism enabled the Myanmar government to deflect international criticism of their anti-Rohingya policies as external interference in domestic affairs, claiming their actions were justifiable.[13]

Ethnography, the systematic study of people and cultures from an insider perspective, is central to anthropology, offering insights that can enhance international mediation efforts. It involves an immersive perspective of communities to understand their lived experiences from their point of view.[14] This approach provides a nuanced understanding of conflicts that can be crucial for mediators seeking culturally sensitive solutions.

In Myanmar's case, an anthropologically informed approach would have overcome cultural relativism by not merely accepting the cultural context which the Myanmar government uses to justify human rights abuses, but by also engaging with the Rohingya and other ethnic communities to uncover and address the deeper cultural issues underlying the conflict. This balanced approach would respect cultural diversity while addressing human rights violations, demonstrating anthropology's essential role in effective international mediation.

Effectively navigating these twin dangers of cultural imperialism and cultural relativism thus requires mediators to adopt an anthropological approach that acknowledges the cultural complexities of conflicts while addressing ethical concerns inherent in mediation contexts.

IV. International Relations Mediation Tactics Informed by Adoption of Local Communication Frameworks (Rituals)

Anthropologists are interested in ways socio-cultural factors influence the subjective experience of humans. This intersects with cognitive neuroscience which investigates the neural underpinnings and consequences of social experience. In the context of rituals, from a neuroscience perspective, such a cultural phenomenon involves stimulation, making it a major contributor to its role as a central mechanism of socialisation. The unique features of rituals lend themselves to associative learning, imbuing social ideologies with significance to individuals identifying with the culture. Thus, the link of rituals to emotions allows them to be motivationally salient. Mediation can leverage this aspect of biological anthropology to create successful outcomes.[15]

The Bougainville Peace Process highlights the anthropological and neuroscientific significance of rituals in conflict resolution. Rituals played a crucial role in reconciling grievances stemming from environmental degradation and economic impacts caused by the Panguna mine in Papua New Guinea. The controversies surrounding the mine and its impact on national identity sparked an armed rebellion in 1988, which led to a decade-long civil war.

The peace process organised by the New Zealand government, also known as Burnham I and II, laid the foundations for a successful truce, ending the civil war by specifically utilising a non-Western framework. Delegates eschewed a traditional negotiation table and addressed issues after confidence-building exercises involving indigenous customs such as traditional songs and traditional Maori greeting ceremonies. The government's explicit acknowledgement of indigenous customs resonated strongly with local communities.

Additionally, *Taraut* sessions also allowed the indigenous community to express their grievances in their own cultural practices, and to resolve any conflicts they had in a way probably unusual to the typical Western mediation framework. The fact that it resonated with the indigenous community was a big reason why it worked and the Burnham Truce was eventually signed, marking the end of the conflict.[16] The Bougainville Peace Process leveraged local communication frameworks (rituals), validating the importance of anthropologically informed approaches in achieving successful mediation outcomes.

V. Successful Jus Post Bellum by Considering The Anthropological Impact of War

Just War Theory provides a framework for understanding when violence may be morally justified and how peace can be ethically restored.[17] A real-life example of a successful way where post-war justice (Jus Post Bellum) was restored through consideration of an anthropological perspective is the Agent Orange resolution that took place after the Vietnam War. Compensation for the effects of Agent Orange is intertwined with anthropological principles as it addresses the long-term socio-cultural and health impacts of the chemical on affected populations.

Vietnam's Red Cross has estimated that to date, around three million people suffered inheritable genetic ailments from Agent Orange, a chemical defoliant sprayed by the United States forces across Vietnam during the war. The United States Agency for International Development (USAID) facilitated compensation by cleaning up the poisonous dioxin left by the chemical at the airport in the city of Da Nang. Addressing these adverse impacts through compensation involved acknowledging the suffering and taking concrete steps to make amends, and was instrumental in rebuilding trust between the United States and Vietnam.[18]

VI. Acknowledging Historical Narratives to Achieve Restorative Justice

Intervention in terms of settlements and truces does not simply erase lasting tears in the social fabric of intercultural relations. An anthropologically conscious perspective has to be considered when mediating ethnic grievances in the long run.

For example, Rwanda's historical tensions between the Hutu and Tutsi communities are steeped in deep-rooted ethnic and political complexities that were eventually catalysed into the 1994 Rwanda genocide. Tutsis historically view their role as leaders under King Rwabugiri who created *Uburetwa,* which required Hutu peasants to provide labour in exchange for access to land, while Tutsis were largely exempted. Belgian colonisers further entrenched this hegemony by employing policies that favoured the Tutsi aristocracy.

On the other hand, Hutus see themselves as oppressed and exploited by the Tutsi-dominated feudal system and colonial policies that entrenched Tutsi privilege. The Hutu Revolution was a justified struggle to overthrow an unjust Tutsi-dominated monarchy. These deep-seated historical grievances eventually imploded in 1994, when the Hutu President's plane was shot down. Fuelled by ethnic grievances, a radical Hutu radio channel announced his demise, urging Hutus to attack the Tutsi population as retribution, marking the start of the genocide.[19]

Over 100 days in 1994, an estimated 800,000 Rwandans were slaughtered by Hutu extremists,[20] impacting Rwandan ethnic relations in a devastating way. In post-genocide Rwanda, international mediators had to navigate the bloodshed-steeped wake of strained relations between the Hutus and Tutsis. Addressing grievances, acknowledging historical injustices, and promoting reconciliation required a deep understanding of these narratives to build sustainable peace.

The UN had passed Resolution 912 withdrawing most peacekeepers, leaving a symbolic presence of 270 soldiers due to the instability of the region, rendering it unsafe for peacekeeping.[21] UN resolutions in the context of the Rwanda genocide seemed to be a mere Band-Aid and were unable to address complex ethnic grievances, and were even overwhelmed by the intensity of the violence resulting from the complicated narratives and deep-seated resentment between the differing communities.

In contrast, the Gacaca Courts in Rwanda employed restorative justice principles, emphasising reconciliation over punitive measures to resolve conflict and promote healing for survivors. The government made this traditional restorative justice approach accessible in every community, aiming to address the limitations of retributive justice and international resolutions by fostering truth-telling and initiating an apology-forgiveness cycle among victims and perpetrators. This facilitated a community healing process, enabling survivors to share their narratives and be informed of the whereabouts of their deceased relatives as a form of closure. This was a pivotal mechanism for justice and reconciliation in Rwanda's post-conflict society.[22]

Integrating anthropologically informed mediation, such as community courts, alongside UN resolutions, can effectively stop violence and provide immediate justice. While UN resolutions focus on short-term conflict resolution, mediation in community courts are more effective at addressing deep-seated grievances and fostering long-term peace through reconciliation.

VII. Anthropology Colours Mediators

A fundamental principle of mediation is that the third-party mediator must ensure a fair consensus. However, it would be idealistic to assume that international mediator organisations are totally unbiased and neutral. Like the countries they mediate for, these mediators operate within complex cultural dynamics and historical narratives of their own, inherently influencing their mediation practices. This can be seen clearly in the international mediation efforts with regard to the Israel-Palestine conflict.

Both Israel and Palestine assert legitimate justifications for their conflict: Israel often cites its right to self-defence against attacks from militant groups, while Palestine argues for its right to resist occupation and achieve self-determination. According to the Just War Theory, war must be declared by a legitimate authority. However, this criterion is contentious in the Israel-Palestine conflict, as both sides question the legitimacy of the other's governing bodies. Both nations believe they have an absolute rightful claim to the same land based on religious doctrine.

The Peel Commission in 1937 and the United Nations in 1947 proposed dividing the land between Jewish and Arab residents of Palestine.

This created a grey area that bred conflict since international organisations recognised the claims of both peoples to the land.[23] The clashing narratives of both communities have made it challenging to achieve a lasting mediation.

International mediators involved in the conflict have biases, with Western mediators leaning towards being pro-Israel due to shared history. Mediation efforts between Israel and Palestine have fallen short due to biases stemming from such anthropological differences in how the international actors relate to Israel.

When modern Israel was founded in 1948, the United States was among the first to recognise the country, influenced by a shared identity of being nations founded on democracy and freedom. During the Cold War, Israel was seen as a strategic ally of the United States, and crucial because of Soviet influence in the Middle East. The United States provided immense military and financial support to bolster Israel's position.[24] The bias of the United States towards Israel has continued to this day and can be seen prominently in initiatives like the Trump administration's "Peace to Prosperity" plan in 2020. This envisioned a two-state solution with significant concessions favouring Israel, recognising Israeli sovereignty over major settlements and acknowledging Jerusalem as Israel's capital. In contrast, under the same plan, Palestinians would only be granted a form of statehood with restrictions.[25]

Unsurprisingly, the plan was seen by Palestinians as inherently biased towards Israeli interests. From an anthropological standpoint, this solution disregards the symbolic attachments Palestinians have to East Jerusalem, undermining the feasibility of such a compromise. It is hence not a surprise that Trump's attempted mediation was not successful.

VIII. The Way Forward — Anthropologically Informed Mediation

A. *Ethnographic fieldwork*

International mediators often propose blanket resolutions, as exemplified by the Trump's administration's plan. This is limiting as it disregards cultural narratives. Ethnographic fieldwork, a key tenet of anthropology, sheds light on nuances of community sentiments and insights from this fieldwork could eventually lead to a more culturally satisfactory outcome for both parties. The study of landscapes reflects the sociopolitical dynamics of Israel-Palestine, where Israeli geographers transformed symbolic claims into material possessions as the nation of Israel.

Conversely, Palestinian geographers highlight the erasure of Palestinian communities, from the 1948 Nakba to current settlement expansions in Jerusalem and the West Bank, and how Palestinians feel like their homeland is being occupied by Israeli settlers.[26] This insight could have better informed the Trump's administration's plan, which overlooked Palestinian cultural sensitivities with regards to Jerusalem's status.

B. *Fostering dialogue*

Intercultural dialogues are in no way a definite means to guarantee conflict resolution, but scheduled and consistent dialogues over time can yield eventual progress in mediation. By allowing each culture to understand the other's perspective, common ground can be found. More dialogues could be held between the Israeli and Palestinian communities, mirroring the successful Northern Ireland Peace Process.

The current conflict between Israel and Palestine parallels that the conflict between the Catholics and Protestants of Northern Ireland as both conflicts involve almost irreconcilable culture differences, thus making Northern Ireland's successful dialogue approach potentially applicable to Israel-Palestine. In Northern Ireland, identity is closely tied to religious affiliation (Protestant vs. Catholic) and political allegiance (unionist vs. nationalist). These identities are reinforced by historical narratives and perceptions of rights.

The conflict in Northern Ireland, often referred to as "The Troubles", was a complex ethno-nationalist and political conflict between the unionist Protestant community, who identified with British sovereignty and wished to remain part of the United Kingdom ("**UK**"), and the nationalist Catholic community, who sought a united Ireland independent of British rule.[27] These communities have almost irreconcilable differences, similar to Israel and Palestine's clashing historical, geographical, and national interests.

The Northern Ireland peace process began with dialogues in the late 1980s. By the early 1990s, these interactions had led to a broader political engagement, culminating in the Good Friday Agreement of 1998. The agreement gave formal recognition to Northern Ireland's multiple identities, allowing residents to identify as British, Irish or both. It ended direct rule by the UK and set up a Northern Ireland legislature and a power-sharing government model between unionist and nationalist parties.[28] These dialogues were crucial in transforming the political landscape in Northern Ireland, demonstrating the vital role of sustained communication and engagement to achieve peace. The agreement established power-sharing arrangements and mechanisms for cross-community cooperation, contributing to decades of relative peace in the region.[29]

This approach can be applied to the Israeli-Palestinian conflict, as understanding each side's historical narrative is crucial for fostering peace, and this could be achieved through open dialogues. Mutual acknowledgement of historical perspectives could also promote moderation in the present and future. The goal of such a dialogue is not to resolve the clashing historical narratives completely, but rather to facilitate mutual respect and understanding in the Israeli-Palestinian conflict. With acknowledgement of each other's differing perspectives, a solution that is the best compromise for both sides regarding contested issues like the status of Jerusalem can be more effectively reached.[30]

IX. Conclusion

In Ruth Benedict's words, "The purpose of anthropology is to make the world safe for human differences".[31] Anthropological insights are indispensable in understanding the complex dynamics and existing differences between conflicting cultural identities.

In the realm of international relations mediation, it also illuminates the biases of international relations mediators, revealing the tendency to lean towards seeing conflicts in stark black-and-white terms, overlooking the intricate shades of grey encompassing complex cultural dynamics. Anthropology provides a lens through which international relations mediation can evolve to address these complex cultural dimensions.

By embracing ethnographic methods, historical awareness, and local communication frameworks, mediators can design interventions that are effective, equitable and culturally attuned. By integrating anthropological insights into mediation processes, we can better navigate these complexities, fostering more nuanced and culturally informed approaches to conflict resolution.

https://doi.org/10.1142/9789819825042_0010

Chapter 10

Charting Twin Pursuits — Reconciling the Tension Between Confidentiality as a Procedural Feature and the State's Interest in Pursuing Transparency in Mediating Investor-State Disputes

Ng Xin Yu

I. Introduction

The Confucian adage "No wisdom like silence" reflects the value of remaining silent. In a similar vein, it has been suggested that silence is valued even during mediation — where frank communication is prioritised — insofar as what transpires in the mediation process would remain confidential.[1] Confidentiality has been deemed a "central tenet and precondition of mediation",[2] differentiating mediation from other means of alternative dispute resolution ("**ADR**").[3,4] This core procedural feature is also regarded as an essential element for successfully mediating disputes.[5]

However, where investor-state disputes concern matters of public interest and involve the government, the need for transparency is more acute,[6–8] given the general perception that a democratic state should be subject to public scrutiny.[9] In fact, since good governance entails transparency and public participation,[10,11] the lack of transparency in investor-state dispute settlement ("**ISDS**") is often criticised.[12] Such considerations are similarly reflected in the deliberations of the United Nations Commission on International Trade Law ("**UNCITRAL**") Working Group III regarding the relevance of transparency reforms in ISDS.[13]

In this regard, the inherent tension between confidentiality and transparency[14] raises the following question: to what extent can the procedural feature of confidentiality in mediation be reconciled with the pursuit of transparency in resolving investor-state disputes? To this end, it is posited that confidentiality can be harmonised with the need for transparency in investor-state mediation ("**ISM**"). Notwithstanding certain obstacles to reconciling these seemingly competing interests, it is prudent to approach the confidentiality-transparency debate with renewed perspectives that best reflect the current and future development of ISM.

II. Roadmap

This paper will first address some preliminary considerations (Section II). Following an examination of how the parallel aims of confidentiality and transparency may be achieved in ISM (Section III), this paper will explore how these principles may be further reconciled moving forward (Section IV) before concluding (Section V).

III. Preliminary Considerations

A. *Confidentiality in mediation and what it entails*

Confidentiality in mediation is threefold, comprising "insider–outsider confidentiality, insider–insider confidentiality, and insider–court confidentiality".[15] Pertinently, insider-outsider confidentiality imposes a duty on all participants to refrain from making "prohibited disclosures" to individuals who are not parties to the mediation, unless expressly permitted by exceptions to confidentiality.[16] Such disclosures may pertain to the information exchanged during the mediation, the announcement of mediation occurring, the admissibility of mediation documents in other proceedings, and the resultant settlement agreement.[17,18] The confidentiality principle is equally applied in the context of ISM.[19]

B. *A state's considerations and interests in ISM*

In investor-state disputes, which often present politically sensitive issues,[20] parties are chiefly concerned with confidentiality and procedural flexibility in opting for a particular means of dispute resolution.[21–23] State officials prioritise the cost- and time-efficiency of dispute settlement, along with the desire to retain control over outcomes and maintain lasting partnerships.[24]

Mediation effectively addresses these interests of states, namely, the desire for confidentiality, procedural flexibility, time-cost efficiency, control over outcomes and the preservation of long-term relationships. Correspondingly, the rising appeal of mediation as a form of ADR,[25] including within the context of ISDS, is significant.[26] As mediation emphasises reaching settlements based on mutual consent, this gives effect to a state's legitimate policy considerations, thereby circumscribing the risk of non-compliance with any resulting settlement agreement. ISM addresses the policy costs of binding arbitral decisions ordering a host state to reverse "measures that were implemented for the public good".[27] The focus of mediation on extra-legal interests, and its potential for maintaining amicable relations, further preserves the symbiotic relationship between a state and investors.[28]

At the same time, states seek certainty and predictability in dispute resolution as rules-based entities.[29] Notwithstanding the alignment of ISM to a state's interests as discussed above, it has been further suggested that states may be hesitant to attempt ISM due to concerns about public accountability.[30] Government officials are less incentivised, even averse, to facilitate an agreement to a mediation settlement since it may be publicly perceived as a product of corruption or inept government function if the outcome overly favours the investors.[31] This is supported by empirical evidence reflecting that officials are unwilling to bear public responsibility due to fears of potential prosecution for alleged corruption, public criticism, and setting precedents for compensation.[32]

C. *Research scope*

In light of how a state is perceived to be the party being more reluctant to settle in investor-state disputes,[33] this paper will explore the confidentiality-transparency debate from a state's standpoint. This serves to examine how reconciling these twin aims would address a state's underlying concerns regarding ISM as set out above.

Further, this paper primarily considers the insider–outsider aspect of confidentiality as the demands for transparency are most prevalent among external parties. In evaluating ISM, where appropriate, views regarding transparency reforms in investor-state arbitration ("**ISA**") will also be considered.

IV. A Critical Examination of How Confidentiality and Transparency Can Be Balanced in ISM

A. *Reconciling the procedural safeguard of confidentiality and the need for transparency*

(1) *Harnessing the benefits of confidentiality to address a state's interests*

At the outset, it is important to dispel the notion that confidentiality and secrecy necessarily have negative connotations.[34] Confidentiality remains desirable for resolving investor-state disputes through ISM. It provides a sense of security by protecting strategic secrets to the advantage of both the state and the investor.[35] The International Centre for Settlement of Investment Disputes ("**ICSID**") recognised the value of confidentiality in allowing the parties to engage freely and creatively.[36] Moreover, as observed by the UNCITRAL Working Group II, "requiring parties to provide information about their disputes might inadvertently exacerbate [their] differences".[37]

Indeed, without the procedural guarantee of confidentiality, mediation ceases to be practicable.[38] Crucially, as reforms for increasing transparency standards in ISA are implemented,[a] this guarantee confers mediation with a relative advantage *vis-à-vis* arbitration as a greater degree of confidentiality increases the likelihood of settlement at mediation.[39]

It bears noting that strict confidentiality is the condition which maximises the advantages of ISM through promoting candour,[40] as sensitive

---

[a] Such transparency requirements were introduced by the UNCITRAL Rules on Transparency in Treaty-based Investor-State arbitration, and the United Nations Convention on Transparency in Treaty-Based Investor-State Arbitration (Mauritius Convention). See UNCITRAL Rules on Transparency in Treaty-based Investor-State Arbitration (2014), as adopted by Resolution of the General Assembly 68/109, U.N. Doc. A/68/462 (Dec. 16, 2013), <www.uncitral.org/pdf/english/texts/arbitration/rules-on-transparency/Rules-on-Transparency-E.pdf>

information may only be addressed effectively without "excessive interference from media and public opinion".[41] In response to the need to resolve polycentric issues,[42] ISM retains the potential to address diverging interests of stakeholders in evolving disputes.[43]

A brief survey of general procedural rules governing ISM reveals the longstanding centrality of confidentiality. Such rules often adopt a default position of confidentiality,[44] where information relating to, and documents prepared for the mediation are strictly confidential unless disclosure is legally required or agreed upon by parties.[45] Certain rules stipulate that the very administration of the mediation is similarly confidential.[46] This observable adherence to confidentiality in ISM evidences its sustained relevance, notwithstanding the differing degrees of specificity in various confidentiality and disclosure provisions under their respective institutional regimes. Moreover, very few states have stressed the need to heighten transparency in mediation proceedings during ICSID consultation.[47] Other institutional guidelines reveal the need to preserve confidentiality in ISM even when considering the countervailing need for transparency.[48]

Further, on a domestic level, confidentiality provisions are similarly incorporated into a state's governance of investment-related mediation proceedings. This is seen in China's approach to consensual settlement as reflected in its establishment of an extensive ADR network for ISDS.[49,50] Notably, the Chinese Ministry of Commerce introduced the *Rules on Handling Complaints of Foreign Invested Enterprises* for managing investment disputes, providing safeguards for maintaining the confidentiality of proceedings and parties' information.[51,52]

Given the paramount importance of upholding confidentiality in mediation, it is not in and of itself at odds with a state's interest when relying on ISM. Consistent adherence to confidentiality will not preclude any effort to achieve transparency, as will be discussed in the following section.

(2) *Transparency can be achieved without compromising confidentiality entirely*

As an equally significant counterweight to confidentiality, transparency may still be pursued while preserving the confidentiality of mediation proceedings. This is crucial for ensuring the credibility of the mediation process,[53] and the legitimacy of ISDS.[54] Precedents of non-confidential public sector resource mediation demonstrate the potential for transparency to feature in certain ISM cases.[55]

To illustrate, a public mediation process was adopted in the 1987 Snake River Basin case, where the dispute involved over 150,000 water rights claims.[56] The hybrid arrangement of public meetings, private meetings, expert meetings, seminars, and a variety of exchanges of information between the various stakeholders,[57] was arguably necessary in such a large-scale ISM.

Further, procedural rules reveal the potential for balancing confidentiality and transparency. For instance, Article 10 of the International Bar Association Rules for Investor-State Mediation safeguards the confidentiality of the mediation proceeding itself and sensitive documents but promotes transparency as to the outcome among other specified types of information. Additionally, a single mediation case is reported to have been administered by the International Chamber of Commerce thus far.[58]

In *Systra SA v. Republic of the Philippines*, it was revealed that the parties did not reach an eventual settlement, but the process was cost-effective and instrumental in facilitating communication despite initial difficulties in securing the parties' participation.[59] Disclosure of such information deemed non-sensitive by parties would assist potential users, including other states, in assessing the suitability of mediation for future investor-state disputes.

To this end, transparency reforms in ISA may be relevant for ISM, as it may facilitate greater predictability and consistency across the outcomes of ISDS cases.[60] As part of the UNCITRAL Working Group III's deliberations,[61] transparency was emphasised as a "key element of the rule of law, and of access to justice as well as legitimacy on ISDS". It further recognised a need to distinguish between transparency of arbitration and a broader notion of transparency.[62] This conception of transparency would be implemented for "all types of dispute resolution proceedings initiated pursuant to [the mechanism identified in respective international investment agreements]".[63] Accordingly, the potential for reforms provides an opportunity for reevaluating the balance between confidentiality and transparency in ISM.

(3) *Calibrating the requisite levels of confidentiality and transparency*

In this regard, confidentiality and transparency are not necessarily conflicting, especially considering how full transparency and public participation may jeopardise a state's interests in ISM.[64] In fact, transparency impedes mediation efforts by exposing early stages of discussions to public scrutiny which may engender posturing and unproductive dialogue.[65]

Granted, the confidentiality of ISM may not be compatible with the need for citizens' control over settlements in cases involving fundamental rights.[66] However, the suitability of ADR for investor-state disputes must be carefully examined in the first instance, since in certain circumstances, a sovereign state should not be permitted to compromise on public interest laws and make concessions for investors.[67] Thus, this indicates the need for calibrating the degree of transparency required for each investor-state dispute, and at various stages of the mediation process, rather than introducing sweeping transparency reforms for all categories of ISM.

B. *Navigating the outstanding challenges presented by the confidentiality-transparency tension*

(1) *Unresolved issues regarding the lack of transparency hinder a state from reconciling its competing aims*

At this juncture, it must be noted that even if confidentiality coheres with a state's interests, this does not detract from the need to tackle outstanding concerns stemming from limited transparency.

Pertinently, there remains a perceived risk that states may rely on ISM to shield disputes from public scrutiny and debate, thereby circumventing the need for transparency entirely.[68,69] Immunity from public scrutiny may threaten the very integrity of the process.[70] This is evinced by the scepticism of civil society or the general citizenry, as another stakeholder in ISDS, towards ISM due to the higher degree of confidentiality involved.[71]

Such overriding concerns of public perception are especially pressing in the context of investor-state disputes, as the settlement may contravene principles of good governance, which entail ensuring government accountability and respecting the rights of citizens.[72] Without transparency, the very flexibility in option generation as provided by mediation may result in reduced levels of accountability and legitimacy, in turn causing complexities at the enforcement stage.[73]

Corollary issues arise from the limited transparency of mediation, which may engender future obstacles for a state when the need for ISM arises. First, confidentiality may prevent a more diverse pool of qualified third-party mediator appointments since the requisite expertise and experience in ISM would remain within closed circles. Second, confidential ISM runs counter to "efforts to increase predictability and consistency between the outcomes of investor-state disputes", where resultant inconsistencies may in turn exacerbate inequity.[74] The exact number and frequency of ISM cases remain elusive precisely due to confidentiality.[75] These shortcomings of confidential ISM effectively prevent a state from fully utilising ISM, resulting in a vicious cycle where ISM continues to be relatively underutilised for resolving investor-state disputes.[76]

(2) *Rethinking the approach to confidentiality and transparency in ISM*

Nevertheless, it is posited that such implications may be mitigated by adapting ISM to the dynamic needs of parties. Moving away from the zero-sum paradigm, it has been suggested that the core feature of confidentiality can be retained with the disclosure of select information. This includes announcing the preparation for or commencement of mediation, which serves to inform civil society stakeholders or affected third parties.

Having regard to the need for transparency in ISM, the scope of confidentiality exceptions can be widened to maintain "a level of transparency somewhere between that of commercial mediation and that of investment arbitration".[77] In this respect, the exceptions to transparency in ISA could be similarly adopted in ISM.[78] Parties' consent to any form of disclosure is still required.[79]

To further assuage concerns regarding the complete erosion of confidentiality in mediation in general, a bifurcation of transparency rules may be applied for commercial mediation and ISM respectively, such that a separate regime for ISM may better reflect the need for a relatively higher degree of transparency. Crucially, it is asserted that automatic transparency,[80] should not be the default position lest the essence of confidentiality in mediation is lost. Instead, confidentiality and privacy should be preserved to an appreciable degree.[81]

Even if transparency reforms are implemented for ISM, documents and points raised in mediation should still be kept confidential even if the case is eventually arbitrated or litigated.[82] This enables a moderate improvement of transparency for what is essentially still a confidential process, which also assists in increasing the visibility of ISM among its potential users.[83]

Ultimately, the underlying concern regarding secrecy of ISM stems from the very opacity of proceedings. However, if a state can keep the public apprised of the ISM in question by issuing joint disputant communiqués, it can effectively achieve the objective of publicising the important public work being performed.[84] Thus, with the potential recalibration of the requisite level of transparency required in ISM, states may still reconcile the seemingly diverging aims of achieving greater transparency for matters of public interest and protecting its strategic interests behind closed doors.

V. Further Evaluation: A Way Forward?

In light of the foregoing analysis, the apparent conflict between confidentiality and transparency may not be entirely irreconcilable. On the one hand, the two aims, while conceptually contrasting, are not mutually exclusive. The benefits of mediation as protected by confidentiality cannot be overlooked, whereas full transparency is neither necessary nor beneficial for addressing a state's interests. On the other hand, outstanding issues arising from the lack of transparency seemingly render the confidentiality-transparency debate irreconcilable. Nevertheless, this does not preclude harmonising both goals through suitable reforms.

At this relatively nascent stage of development where the effectiveness of ISM has not yet been systematically tested,[85] confidentiality ought to be preserved robustly to promote its unique value proposition. This is because despite concerted efforts to promote the use of mediation to resolve investor-state disputes, ISM remains underutilised.[86] Interest-based approaches to ISDS are deemed less effective when relied upon independently, than when utilised in tandem with other rights-based approaches to dispute resolution.[87]

However, academic sentiment tentatively suggests that as ISM progressively develops, and with cases being published with parties' consent, the pursuit of transparency could be re-examined with an eye toward gradual openness in the long term.[88] Indeed, parties are warming to the idea of settling investor-state disputes amicably,[89] despite the prevalence of ISA. Nearly one-fifth of bilateral investment treaties ("**BITs**") contain provisions for mediation or conciliation,[90] and model BITs similarly promote such forms of dispute resolution mechanisms. Recent developments such as the adoption of the Convention on International Settlement Agreements Resulting from Mediation,[91] and the 2022 ICSID Mediation Rules,[92] are reasons for optimism that ISM has evolved,[93] and will continue to be promulgated.

In any event, it might be useful to recognise confidentiality and transparency as complementary guiding principles, rather than absolute aims. This would introduce a paradigm shift in this balancing act, and be a better response to a state's multi-faceted considerations. For instance, as numerous ministries are often involved in investment treaty disputes, measures are required to ensure that confidentiality is duly observed by the officials across ministries.[94] Concurrently, inter-ministerial decision-making may necessitate consultations with parties external to the mediation.

In accordance with these principles, guidelines may be implemented. For instance, the International Mediation Institute Competency Criteria for Investor-State Mediators emphasises the need for mediators conducting ISM to address the needs of transparency and media correspondence, and that of confidentiality and building trust.[95]

To increase public legitimacy of the eventual settlement, the International Energy Charter Guide on Investment Mediation recommends that states may adopt an internal monitoring system where representatives regularly report to officials on the mediation progress for continuous accountability. It further proposes that states disclose the fact that mediation is occurring and the key settlement points through a single spokesperson.[96] These proposals highlight the practical possibility of reconciling confidentiality and transparency in ISM, which is valuable for a state's consideration.

VI. Conclusion

Confidentiality and transparency are but two sides of the same coin. While transparency appears to be antithetical to the mediation process, states must weigh the need for public accountability and credibility against its interests in resolving investor-state disputes discreetly where appropriate.

Indeed, efforts to harmonise the conflicting interests reveal both the potential for succeeding in this balancing act, and the resolve of stakeholders to do so. Remaining cognisant of how total transparency would obviate the essence of mediation, it is thus more important to strike a delicate balance between the duty of transparency and the right to confidentiality as the visibility of ISM increases.

https://doi.org/10.1142/9789819825042_0011

Chapter 11

The Risk of Settlement Regret: A Critical Factor in Counsel's Decision-Making Process?[a]

Tay Theng Shuen

I. Introduction

In mediation, seasoned practitioners often quip that "a truly good settlement is one that leaves everyone unhappy".[1] This raises the question of whether the risk of settlement regret — characterised by a lingering dissatisfaction with the settlement outcome — should influence counsel's decisions when advising clients on settlement decisions.

This essay argues that counsel should consider the risk of settlement regret when advising clients on settlement decisions. Lawyers hold considerable influence over their clients' choices and are in a prime position to mitigate against settlement regret by assisting them in making well-informed decisions during the settlement process.

Addressing and mitigating the risks of settlement regret advances the courts' goals of promoting Alternative Dispute Resolution ("**ADR**") to reduce litigation costs and achieve amicable resolutions. A failure to consider such risks could lead to an abuse of court processes or even expose counsel to potential liability for professional negligence. By effectively managing the risk of settlement regret, parties are more likely to reach enduring resolutions with terms that they find satisfactory and are inclined to comply with.

---

[a] I extend my sincere thanks to Danny Quah, Director, CHP Law LLC for his comments and guidance. All mistakes and errors remain mine.

Furthermore, consideration of this risk enables counsel to prioritise the emotional impact of the dispute resolution process on clients and facilitate their pursuit of therapeutic outcomes through mediation more effectively.

Nonetheless, it remains an open question as to whether lawyers should be ethically obligated to consider the risks of settlement regret. While it could be argued that mitigating settlement regret aligns with their ethical obligation to the court, mandating this duty might constrain counsel from fully advocating for their clients' best interests, particularly when the risks of settlement regret are low. Nevertheless, it would be advantageous for counsel to conscientiously evaluate these risks as part of their professional responsibility to act in their clients' best interests.

Potential reforms with regard to a consensual mediation framework could offer better protection against settlement regret for all parties. However, further quantitative research investigating the incidence of settlement regret and qualitative studies exploring how parties are impacted by it would contribute significantly to the discourse on the importance of assessing the risk of settlement regret.

II. What is Settlement Regret?

This essay introduces the term "settlement regret" to denote the lingering dissatisfaction felt by a party following the finalisation of a settlement agreement. Importantly, this sentiment extends beyond mere regret or second-guessing; instead it reflects a deep-seated belief that opting for an alternative course, such as proceeding to trial rather than settling,[2] could have yielded a more favourable result. As a result, clients experiencing this sense of regret may lament their decision, wishing they had either avoided settlement altogether or secured terms more aligned with their expectations and desires.

The ramifications of settlement regret can be multi-faceted. Clients may find themselves revisiting their choices, believing that they compromised excessively or accepted terms that failed to serve their best interests. This lingering dissatisfaction may eventually prompt an action such as attempting to renegotiate the settlement informally, breaching the agreement, or even commencing new proceedings to pursue what they perceive as a fairer resolution. Ultimately, settlement regret undermines the intended finality and stability of settlements, and may perpetuate ongoing discord between parties, contrary to the objectives of ADR.

III. Counsel's Pivotal Role in Settlement

Lawyers, as the driving force behind the decisions made during the settlement process, are well-positioned to help mitigate the risks of settlement regret by guiding their clients to make informed choices. Although the negotiating parties themselves are the ones who may experience settlement regret, it is important to remember that they rarely make these decisions in isolation. Most litigants are represented by lawyers, and while clients ultimately have the authority to decide whether to settle a dispute, counsel often exert significant influence over these decisions.[3]

Studies have shown that lawyers are able to persuade litigants to approach the settlement-versus-trial decision from a lawyer's analytical perspective. It follows that lawyers can facilitate settlement in cases when their clients would probably not reach an agreement by themselves.[4] This influence can be attributed to the perception that counsel typically possess significantly greater knowledge about the lawsuit than their clients, and the advantages, if any, of a potential settlement.[5]

During settlement negotiations, counsel may predict potential case outcomes, advise on appropriate settlement offers, and discern which proposals merit acceptance. At times, the weight of counsel's recommendations may even eclipse the client's input, particularly if counsel specialise in that specific area of dispute resolution and are perceived as having received training that could improve their ability to make sound judgements.[6]

Furthermore, lawyers routinely assess settlement offers, and empirical studies indicate that seasoned lawyers tend to offer more precise evaluations of the merits of a case compared to non-legal professionals.[7] Moreover, lawyers often maintain less of an emotional stake in the outcome, enabling them to offer an "outside" or more detached perspective, which to many clients, aid in clear and impartial decision-making.[8]

These factors collectively grant counsel substantial influence in guiding settlement negotiations and directing their clients toward either accepting or rejecting the terms of a settlement agreement. Therefore, the mediating parties' lawyers are ideally positioned to carefully assess and mitigate the risk of settlement regret during the settlement process.

IV. The Objectives of Settlement

Given their great impact on settlement outcomes, it is advantageous for counsel to assess the risk of settlement regret to align with the courts' objectives of promoting ADR to reduce litigation expenses and facilitate sustainable settlements. There have been instances where settlement regret has led parties to initiate proceedings that constituted an abuse of process or exposed counsel to claims of professional negligence. Addressing the risk of settlement regret would undoubtedly increase the likelihood of parties reaching mutually agreeable resolutions that they find satisfactory and will be inclined to honour.

A. *Settlement philosophy according to the judiciary*

Addressing and mitigating the risks of settlement regret aligns closely with the judiciary's original rationale for promoting ADR methods in the 1990s: to provide cost-effective, less adversarial alternatives to litigation, manage judicial caseloads, and foster communal values through amicable settlements.[9]

As mediation and other ADR practices were gradually introduced in Singapore,[10] the legal framework evolved to support prompt, binding resolutions outside the courtroom, guided by the principle that litigation should be a last resort.[11] The establishment of the Singapore Mediation Centre in 1997, which provides private commercial mediation services and provides mediator training and accreditation, marked a significant step in institutionalising mediation. Over time, ADR eventually emerged as the preferred primary method for resolving disputes.[12]

B. *Codifying the mandatory requirement to undergo ADR*

In 2022, the Rules of Court 2021 ("**ROC 2021**") came into operation and introduced a presumption in favour of ADR with the aim of fostering fair, efficient, and cost-effective dispute resolution. Under Order 5 of the ROC

2021, litigants are required to pursue amicable resolutions before and during legal actions or appeals. The court may compel parties to undergo ADR unless they opt out, and refusal to attempt ADR must be justified in a sealed document, which is only reviewed if costs are contested. Additionally, the court is empowered to issue cost orders in cases of unreasonable refusals. Similarly, under the State Courts Practice Directions 2021 ("**SCPD**"), litigants must select an ADR method or justify their decision to opt out.[13]

Under the current framework, while parties undergoing ADR are not obliged to settle, they must have reasonable grounds for refusing to attempt an amicable resolution. However, when there is a genuine risk of clients experiencing settlement regret due to dissatisfaction or uncertainty about settling, achieving an amicable resolution becomes challenging, let alone ensuring a lasting settlement if one is reached.

C. *Dangers of failing to consider the risk of settlement regret*

Instances of settlement regret can significantly undermine the courts' objectives of encouraging amicable and lasting dispute resolution through ADR. The cases of *Chan Gek Yong v Violet Netto and others*[14] ("***Violet Netto***") and *Johnson v Firth*[15] serve as illustrative examples of how settlement regret may lead to further disputes, either constituting an abuse of process or implicating counsel in claims of professional negligence.

(1) *Further disputes amounting to an abuse of process: Violet Netto*

Notwithstanding the binding and conclusive nature of a mediated settlement agreement ("**MSA**"), the case of *Violet Netto* illustrates how a party's regret over a settlement can lead to proceedings that constitute an abuse of process.

In *Violet Netto*, the appellant contended that an MSA, which stipulated that the respondent would pay her $150,000 in instalments over 17 months, was invalid. This MSA was agreed upon in exchange for the appellant's agreement to drop pending civil suits for professional negligence against the respondent, who had previously represented her in a conveyancing transaction.[16]

One week after the MSA had been finalised, the appellant experienced a change of heart and appeared to backpedal on her obligations under the MSA by indicating an intention to continue with her pending civil suits against the respondent. Eventually, she claimed that the mediators pressured her into signing the agreement and asserted that she was incapacitated and did not fully comprehend the terms.[17]

Ultimately, the Court upheld the validity of the MSA and determined that the appellant reneged on her obligations solely due to dissatisfaction with the instalment arrangements.[18] Importantly, it is evident that failing to address instances of settlement regret can lead to abuse of the court's process, as seen in the appellant's attempt to continue litigating the main suits despite agreeing to the MSA.

(2) *Risks of professional negligence: Johnson v Firth*

The 2021 New South Wales Court of Appeal case of *Johnson v Firth* presents another example of how settlement regret can result in adverse consequences from the standpoint of potential liability on the part of counsel. In this case, the appellant had commenced proceedings against the respondent for damages for professional negligence on the basis that the respondent had settled his claim prematurely and at an undervalue.

The appeal arose from the fact that the respondent had previously represented the appellant in a compensation claim, during which the appellant consistently expressed a desire for an early settlement due to financial hardships.[19] Eventually, he instructed the respondent to settle the claim for $500,000 after an unsuccessful settlement conference.[20] Throughout negotiations, the respondent solicitor had advised the appellant that he could reject the settlement and that he should further contemplate whether to settle as it could be advantageous if he chose not to.[21]

Although the claim was ultimately dismissed, the case turned on the respondent's firm recommendation to the appellant against settling early at a significantly undervalued amount and that the option of delaying the conference was available. Additionally, the court considered the appellant's preference for a swift settlement and inferred that they "would still have accepted the best offer [the respondent] was able to extract in the short term", despite the respondent's advice to wait for an assessment.[22] In this case, the respondent's consideration of his client's potential dissatisfaction with the settlement protected him from a claim that he failed to fulfil his duties as the appellant's legal advisor.

These cases illustrate the importance of counsel proactively evaluating the risk of settlement regret. In practice, legal disputes are complex and shaped by the unique circumstances of each client and case. However, reflecting on instances where settlement regret led to abuses of process and allegations of professional negligence against counsel, it becomes evident that proactive evaluation and mitigation of settlement regret are advantageous for both counsel and clients.

This approach would enhance the likelihood of achieving enduring resolutions that leave clients satisfied with settlement outcomes, particularly when parties opt for settlement. Consequently, it diminishes the occurrence of non-compliance or disputes arising from regret, aligning with the courts' objectives of promoting ADR.

V. Enhancing the Therapeutic Outcomes of Mediation

The proposition that acknowledging the risk of settlement regret would facilitate amicable and enduring resolutions is supported by the recognition that settlement regret constitutes a negative emotional experience that can profoundly impact clients. The settlement process is often mentally and emotionally challenging for all parties, and by addressing and mitigating the risk of regret, counsel can gain a better understanding of their clients' emotional needs and empower them to assert their preferences in the settlement process. This approach enables clients to pursue therapeutic outcomes through mediation more effectively, thereby enhancing the probability of achieving lasting and amicable settlements.

There are clear links between parties' emotional states and their perceptions of how mediation is progressing.[23] Parties are more likely to comply with and feel satisfied by settlement agreements if they perceive that due process was given and that the mediation outcome was fair.[24] This perception of fairness often takes precedence over the importance of securing a favourable offer.[25]

These concepts of procedural fairness and due process fall under the umbrella of therapeutic jurisprudence ("**TJ**"), which acknowledges the "human element" of the law and advocates for its potential to have therapeutic and anti-therapeutic impacts on individuals' lives.[26,27]

TJ principles are increasingly integrated into various legal practice areas today, particularly in family law, where the objective of settlement has expanded beyond legal outcomes to encompass long-term emotional and relational restoration. This is achieved through a focus on counsel developing a comprehensive holistic understanding of their client's needs, promoting client self-determination, and establishing trusting relationships with them.[28]

Family law is often seen as particularly suited to a TJ approach due to its highly emotional and relational nature, where acrimony between parties can impede resolution.[29,30] However, regardless of the legal context of the dispute, when there is a potential for settlement regret, counsel should consider encouraging parties to openly discuss their concerns, issues, and emotional triggers during mediation. This approach is integral to effectively alleviating the negative emotions tied to the dispute resolution process, and will provide the impetus towards resolution or cooperation.

VI. Is There an Ethical Obligation to Consider the Risk of Settlement Regret?

Despite the compelling arguments presented regarding the benefits of factoring in the risk of settlement regret, it remains an open question as to whether lawyers' ethical duties should include consideration of such risks.

Addressing the risk of settlement regret could be viewed as forming part of lawyers' ethical duty to the court to prevent unnecessary expenses and to avoid wasting judicial resources stemming from clients' regret. However, mandating that counsel must consider and mitigate such risks could potentially limit their ability to effectively pursue their clients' best interests in cases where the risk of settlement regret may not be evident. In navigating such situations, it is beneficial to consider the guiding principles outlined in the Legal Profession (Professional Conduct) Rules 2015 ("**LP(PC)R**").

Under section 5(2)(j) of the LP(PC)R, lawyers have an ethical duty to "use all legal means to advance the client's interests, to the extent that the legal practitioner may reasonably be expected to do so". However, it remains uncertain whether considering the risks of settlement regret should fall within what is "reasonably expected" of lawyers in the course of "advancing the client's interests". This dilemma is particularly relevant in situations where clients are dissatisfied with the settlement or hesitant to settle, despite it being the most advantageous option.

Furthermore, the issue raises the question of who defines the client's interests, whether such interests should be defined by the client or assessed by counsel. In situations where clients opt to settle disputes under objectively less favourable terms, overly emphasising the risk of settlement regret might hinder counsel from effectively advocating for their clients' stated interests.

To some extent, this dilemma is addressed by the guiding principle under section 4(b) of the LP(PC)R that "a legal practitioner's duty to [their] client is subject only to [their] duty to the court". Where the risks of settlement regret are present but remain unacknowledged and unmitigated by counsel, there is a high likelihood of parties breaching the agreed terms or initiating new proceedings to alter them. Consequently, failing to consider the risks of settlement regret could compromise counsel's duty to avoid unnecessary expenses and wasting the court's time (LP(PC)R, 2015, section 55(b)), which ultimately undermines the benefits and goals of settling through ADR.

Clearly, introducing an ethical obligation for counsel to assess the risk of settlement regret would complicate the intricate balance between a lawyer's duty to the court and their responsibility to advocate for their client's best interests. Such an obligation could also unduly restrict counsel from fully pursuing their clients' expressed interests. Moreover, the fact that settlement regret often only manifests after settlement complicates the ethical considerations for counsel in evaluating this risk.

Nonetheless, although not necessarily mandated as an ethical duty for lawyers, the risk of settlement regret deserves significant attention, potentially as a professional obligation throughout counsel's representation. This responsibility becomes especially relevant when clients are hesitant to settle or when settlement terms could result in dissatisfaction.

As illustrated in *Johnson v Firth*, such considerations can also safeguard counsel from potential liability for professional negligence during the course of representation.

VII. Alternative Consent-Based Frameworks

Considering the pitfalls of settlement regret, it might be prudent to re-evaluate the efficacy of mandatory mediation in Singapore. In the United States, scholars have recognised how the legal system, specifically mandatory court-connected mediation programmes, has resulted in instances of "buyer's remorse" and have suggested potential measures for reform to address the dangers of settlement regret. Specifically, they have proposed reforms aimed at improving the quality of justice in these programmes instead of abandoning or discouraging the use of mediation programmes.[31]

One notable suggestion was to emulate the English model, where courts actively encourage mediation without making it mandatory, allowing parties to opt in voluntarily. Similarly, in Singapore, there is merit in shifting the focus towards parties who unreasonably refuse to consent to mediation, rather than penalising those who fail to propose an amicable resolution during compulsory ADR. Considering the multiple factors that could lead to settlement regret and the complexities of mitigating such risks, allowing parties to opt out of the ADR process from the outset could ease the challenges counsel face in addressing the risk of settlement regret.

VIII. Conclusion

The complexities surrounding the risk of settlement regret pose intricate challenges for counsel in conducting and navigating settlement negotiations. Certainly, counsel is optimally positioned to evaluate such risks, and it is imperative that they do so.

This approach not only supports the courts' goals of achieving enduring and amicable resolutions, thereby reducing the likelihood of subsequent disputes that could lead to abuse of process or claims of professional negligence arising from settlement regret, but also promotes therapeutic outcomes in ADR by safeguarding parties' emotional well-being. While managing the risk of settlement regret may aid counsel in fulfilling their duties to the court, these considerations should be viewed as professional responsibilities rather than ethical obligations.

The current system does little to prevent disputants from experiencing settlement regret, and it is posited that allowing parties to participate as consenting agents in the ADR process could be a step toward addressing this issue. Nevertheless, further research into the consequences of disregarding risks associated with settlement regret and the varying experiences of parties affected by it would greatly enrich discussions on the importance of these considerations in maintaining the integrity and objectives of ADR as a therapeutic, non-adversarial alternative to litigation.

https://doi.org/10.1142/9789819825042_bmatter

Endnotes

Chapter 1 Peacemakers: Individuals as Mediators of International Conflicts

1. Whitfield, T. (2010). External actors in mediation: Dilemmas & options for mediators. Geneva: HD Centre for Humanitarian Dialogue.
2. Bercovitch, J., Gartner, SS. (2006). Is there method in the madness of mediation? Some lessons for mediators from quantitative studies of mediation. *Int Interact*, *32*(4):329–54.
3. Zartman, IW., Touval, S. (1985). International mediation: Conflict resolution and power politics. *J Soc Issues*, *41*(2):27–45.
4. Bercovitch, J., Gartner, SS. (2006). Is there method in the madness of mediation? Some lessons for mediators from quantitative studies of mediation. *Int Interact*, *32*(4):329–54.
5. Bercovitch, J., Houston, A. (2000). Why do they do it like this? An analysis of the factors influencing mediation behavior in international conflicts. *J Confl Resolut*, *44*(2):170–202.
6. Zartman, IW., Touval, S. (1985). International mediation: Conflict resolution and power politics. *J Soc Issues*, *41*(2):27–45.
7. Bercovitch, J., Gartner, SS. (2006). Is there method in the madness of mediation? Some lessons for mediators from quantitative studies of mediation. *Int Interact*, *32*(4):329–54.
8. Ibid.
9. Ibid.
10. Ibid.
11. Bercovitch, J., Houston, A. (1993). Influence of mediator characteristics and behaviour on the success of mediation in international relations. *Int J Confl Manag*, *4*(4):297–321.
12. Bercovitch, J., Houston, A. (1996). The study of international mediation: Theoretical issues and empirical evidence. In: *Resolving international conflicts: The theory and practice of mediation*. Boulder, CO: Lynne Rienner Publishers.

13. Bercovitch, J., Gartner, SS. (2006). Is there method in the madness of mediation? Some lessons for mediators from quantitative studies of mediation. *Int Interact*, *32*(4):329–54.
14. Kivimaki, T., Gorman, D. (2008). Non-governmental actors in peace processes: The case of Aceh. Geneva: HD Centre for Humanitarian Dialogue.
15. Ibid.
16. Kingsbury, D. (2006). *Peace in Aceh: A personal accord of the Helsinki peace process*. Jakarta: Equinox Publishing.
17. Ibid.
18. Ibid.
19. Heiling, RM. (2008). Conflict resolution in Aceh in light of track one and a half diplomacy. *Aust J South-East Asian Stud*, *1*(2):171–86.
20. Awaluddin, H. (2008). Why is peace in Aceh successful? [Internet]. London: Conciliation Resources. Available from: http://www.c-r.org/our-work/accord/aceh/success.php
21. Heiling, RM. (2008). Conflict resolution in Aceh in light of track one and a half diplomacy. *Aust J South-East Asian Stud*, *1*(2):171–86.
22. Herrberg, A. (2008). Aceh-Indonesia: The Brussels "backstage" of the Aceh peace process [Internet]. London: Conciliation Resources. Available from: https://www.c-r.org/accord/aceh-indonesia/brussels-backstage-aceh-peace-process
23. Merikallio, K. (2008). *Making peace: Ahtisaari and Aceh*. Juva, Finland: WS Bookwell Oy.
24. Ibid.
25. Ibid.
26. Morfit, M. (2007). The road to Helsinki: The Aceh Agreement and Indonesia's democratic development. *Int Negot*, *12*(1):111–43.
27. Heiling, RM. (2008). Conflict resolution in Aceh in light of track one and a half diplomacy. *Aust J South-East Asian Stud*, *1*(2):171–86.
28. Schulze, KE. (2007). Mission not so impossible: The Aceh Monitoring Mission and lessons learned for the EU. Berlin: Friedrich Ebert Stiftung.
29. Heiling, RM. (2008). Conflict resolution in Aceh in light of track one and a half diplomacy. *Aust J South-East Asian Stud*, *1*(2):171–86.
30. Zartman, IW., Touval, S. (1985). International mediation: Conflict resolution and power politics. *J Soc Issues*, *41*(2):27–45.
31. Curran, D., Sebenius, J. (2003). The mediator as coalition builder: George Mitchell in Northern Ireland. *Int Negot*, *8*(1):111–47.
32. Ibid.

33. Ibid.
34. Ibid.
35. Ibid.
36. Ibid.
37. McWilliams, M., Fearon, K. (1999). Problems of implementation. In: *Accord: Striking a balance: The Northern Ireland peace process*. London: Conciliation Resources.
38. Curran, D., Sebenius, J. (2003). The mediator as coalition builder: George Mitchell in Northern Ireland. *Int Negot*, *8*(1):111–47.
39. Ibid.
40. Ibid.
41. Durkan, M. (1999). The negotiations in practice. In: Accord: *Striking a balance: The Northern Ireland peace process*. London: Conciliation Resources.
42. Duursma, A., Svensson, I. (2019). Introducing an agenda-based measurement of mediation success: The divergent effects of the manipulation strategy in African civil wars. *Int Negot*, *24*(2):296–323.
43. Sisk, TD. (2009). *International mediation in civil wars: Bargaining with bullets*. London: Routledge.
44. Whitfield, T. (2010). External actors in mediation: Dilemmas & options for mediators. Geneva: HD Centre for Humanitarian Dialogue.
45. Sisk, TD. (2009). *International mediation in civil wars: Bargaining with bullets*. London: Routledge.
46. Duursma, A., Svensson, I. (2019). Introducing an agenda-based measurement of mediation success: The divergent effects of the manipulation strategy in African civil wars. *Int Negot*, *24*(2):296–323.
47. Kelman, HC. (2005). Building trust among enemies: The central challenge for international conflict resolution. *Int J Intercult Relat*, *29*(6):639–50.
48. Duursma, A., Svensson, I. (2019). Introducing an agenda-based measurement of mediation success: The divergent effects of the manipulation strategy in African civil wars. *Int Negot*, *24*(2):296–323.

Chapter 2 Advocating for the Narrative Approach to Mediation

1. Monk, G. (1996). Narrative approaches to therapy: The "fourth wave" in family therapy. *Guid Couns, 11*(2):41–7.
2. Hansen, T. (2004). The narrative approach to mediation. *Pepp Disp Resolut Law J.*, *4*(2):297–308.

3. Douglas, S. (2012). Neutrality, self-determination, fairness and differing models of mediation. *James Cook Univ Law Rev., 19*:19–40.
4. Cobb, S. (1994). A narrative perspective on mediation: Toward the materialization of the storytelling metaphor. In: Folger, JP., Jones, TS, editors. *New directions in mediation: Communication research and perspectives.* Thousand Oaks, CA: Sage. p. 48–66.
5. Winslade, J., Monk, G. (2000). *Narrative mediation: A new approach to conflict resolution.* San Francisco, CA: Jossey-Bass.
6. Cobb, S., Rifkin, J. (1991). Neutrality as discursive practice: The construction and transformation of narratives in community mediation. *Stud Law Polit Soc., 11*:69–94.
7. Winslade, J., Monk, G. (2000). *Narrative mediation: A new approach to conflict resolution.* San Francisco, CA: Jossey-Bass.
8. Wylie, H., Paré, DA. (2001). Whose story is it, anyway? An interdisciplinary approach to postmodernism, narrative, and therapy. *Mosaic, 34*(1):153–69.
9. Hansen, T. (2004). The narrative approach to mediation. *Pepp Disp Resolut Law J., 4*(2):297–308.
10. Folger, JP., Poole, MS., Stutman, RK. (2021). *Working through conflict: Strategies for relationships, groups, and organizations.* 9th ed. New York: Routledge.
11. Taylor, A. (2002). *The handbook of family dispute resolution: Mediation theory and practice.* San Francisco, CA: Jossey-Bass.
12. Winslade, J., Monk, G. (2000). *Narrative mediation: A new approach to conflict resolution.* San Francisco, CA: Jossey-Bass.
13. Ibid.
14. Winslade, J., Monk, G., Cotter, A.(1998). A narrative approach to the practice of mediation. *Negot J., 14*(1):21–42.
15. Hansen, T. (2004). The narrative approach to mediation. *Pepp Disp Resolut Law J., 4*(2):297–308.
16. Winslade, J., Monk, G. (2000). *Narrative mediation: A new approach to conflict resolution.* San Francisco, CA: Jossey-Bass.
17. Bush, RAB. (1996). "What do we need a mediator for?: Mediation's 'value-added' for negotiators." *Ohio State J on Disp Resol., 12*:1–36.
18. Hansen, T. (2004). The narrative approach to mediation. *Pepp Disp Resolut Law J., 4*(2):297–308.
19. Douglas, S. (2012). Neutrality, self-determination, fairness and differing models of mediation. *James Cook Univ Law Rev., 19*:19–40.
20. National Mediator Accreditation System. (2008). *Practice standards for NMAS accredited mediators.* Mediator Standards Board.

21. Alexander, NM., Giorgadze, V. (2021). *A handbook on the Singapore Convention on Mediation*. Singapore: Singapore International Dispute Resolution Academy.
22. Cobb, S. (2001). Dialogue and the practice of law and spiritual values: Creating sacred space — Toward a second-generation dispute resolution practice. *Fordham Urban Law J.*, *28*:1017–29.
23. Della Noce, DJ., Bush, RAB., Folger, JP. (2002). Clarifying the theoretical underpinnings of mediation: Implications for practice and policy. *Pepp Disp Resolut Law J.*, *3*(1):39–65.
24. Boulle, L. (2011). *Mediation: Principles, process, practice*. Chatswood, NSW: LexisNexis Butterworths.
25. Douglas, S. (2012). Neutrality, self-determination, fairness and differing models of mediation. *James Cook Univ Law Rev.*, *19*:19–40.
26. Moore, CW (1986). *The mediation process: Practical strategies for resolving conflict*. San Francisco, CA: Jossey-Bass.
27. Coben, JR. (2004). Gollum, meet Smeagol: A schizophrenic rumination on mediator values beyond self-determination and neutrality. *Cardozo J Confl Resol.*, *5*(2):65–86.
28. Douglas, S. (2012). Neutrality, self-determination, fairness and differing models of mediation. *James Cook Univ Law Rev.*, *19*:19–40.
29. Winslade, J., Monk, G. (2000). *Narrative mediation: A new approach to conflict resolution*. San Francisco, CA: Jossey-Bass.
30. Douglas, S. (2012). Neutrality, self-determination, fairness and differing models of mediation. *James Cook Univ Law Rev.*, *19*:19–40.
31. Gunning, IR. (2004). Know justice, know peace: Further reflections on justice, equality, and impartiality in settlement-oriented and transformative mediations. *Cardozo J Confl Resol.*, *5*(2):87–114.
32. Coben, JR. (2004). Gollum, meet Smeagol: A schizophrenic rumination on mediator values beyond self-determination and neutrality. *Cardozo J Confl Resol.*, *5*(2):65–86.
33. Shimokaji, M. The contradiction of mediator neutrality and fairness: A possible solution [Internet]. Mediate.com. [cited 2025 Aug 4]. Available from: https://www.mediate.com/articles/shimokaji.cfm
34. Hyman, J., Love, L. (2002). If Portia were a mediator: An inquiry into justice in mediation. *Clin Law Rev.*, *9*(1):157–93.
35. Ibid.
36. Exon, S. (2008). The effects that mediator styles impose on neutrality and impartiality requirements of mediation. *Univ San Francisco Law Rev.*, *42*:577–620.

37. Shapira, O. (2013). A theory of sharing decision-making in mediation. *McGeorge Law Rev.*, *44*:923–60.
38. Maute, JL. (1990). Mediator accountability: Responding to fairness concerns. *J Disp Resol.*, *1*(2):347–69.
39. Menkel-Meadow, C. (1997). Ethics in ADR representation: A road map of critical issues. *Disp Resol Mag.*, *4*(2):3–6.
40. Lawrence, JKL. (2000). Mediation advocacy: Partnering with the mediator. *Ohio State J on Disp Resol.*, *15*:425–43.
41. Ibid.
42. Ibid.
43. Watkins, M. (1999). Negotiating in a complex world. *Negot J.*, *15*(3): 245–70.
44. Winslade, J., Monk, G. (2000). *Narrative mediation: A new approach to conflict resolution.* San Francisco, CA: Jossey-Bass.
45. Winslade, J., Monk, G. (2000). *Narrative mediation: A new approach to conflict resolution.* San Francisco, CA: Jossey-Bass; Hansen, T. (2004). The narrative approach to mediation. *Pepp Disp Resolut Law J., 4*(2):297–308.

Chapter 3 Beyond the Classroom: Mediation and the Pursuit of Justice

1. Cappelletti, M., Garth, B., Trocker, N. (1976). Access to Justice: Comparative General Report. *The Rabel Journal of Comparative and International Private Law*, *40*, 669–717.
2. Cappelletti, M., Garth, B. (1978). Access to Justice: The Newest Wave in the Worldwide Movement to Make Rights Effective. *Buffalo Law Review, 27(2),* 181–292.
3. de Oliveira, LVP. (2020). To What Degree Should Access to Justice Be Secured in Arbitration? de Oliveira, LVP., Hourani, S., editors (2020). Access to Justice: Concept, Context and Practice. *Kluwer Law International, 7*, 34.
4. Nolan-Haley, J. (2020). International Dispute Resolution and Access to Justice: Comparative Law Perspectives. *Journal of Dispute Resolution, 2,* 391–411.
5. Pickerill, CN. (2007). Specialized Adjudication in an Administrative Forum: Bridging the Gap between Public and Private Law. *Notre Dame Law Review, 82*(4), 1605–1647.

6. McEwen, CA., Williams, L. (1998). Legal Policy and Access to Justice through Courts and Mediation. *Ohio State Journal on Dispute Resolution, 13*, 865–883.
7. United Nations Development Programme. (2005). *Programming for Justice: Access for All: A Practitioner's Guide to Human Rights-Based Approach to Access to Justice.* UNDP
8. Davis, W., Turku, H. (2011). Access to Justice and Alternative Dispute Resolution. *Journal of Dispute Resolution, 1,* 47–65.
9. McEwen, CA., Williams, L. (1998). Legal Policy and Access to Justice through Courts and Mediation. *Ohio State Journal on Dispute Resolution, 13*, 865–883.
10. Cappelletti, M., Garth, B. (1978). Access to Justice: The Newest Wave in the Worldwide Movement to Make Rights Effective. *Buffalo Law Review, 27*(2),181–292.
11. Nolan-Haley, J. (2020.) International Dispute Resolution and Access to Justice: Comparative Law Perspectives. *Journal of Dispute Resolution, 2,* 391–411.
12. Cooley, JW. (1996). *Mediation Advocacy (NITA's Practical Guide Series).* Louisville, CO: National Institute for Trial Advocacy.
13. United Nations Commission on International Trade Law. (2020). *International Commercial Mediation: Draft UNCITRAL Notes on Mediation.* UNCITRAL. Available from: https://documents-dds-ny.un.org/doc/UNDOC/GEN/V20/000/23/PDF/V2000023.pdf?OpenElement
14. De Palo, G., D'Urso, L. (2016). *Achieving a Balanced Relationship between Mediation and Judicial Proceedings.* Directorate-General for Internal Policies, European Parliament.
15. Davar, BS. (2020) ADR and Access to Justice: Perspectives from the UK. *The Law Review Anthology.* Available from: https://lawanthology.com/2020/07/31/adr-and-access-to-justice-perspectives-from-the-uk/
16. Mendez-Pinedo, ME. (2011). Access To Justice As Hope In The Dark: In Search For A New Concept In European Law. *International Journal of Humanities and Social Science, 19*(1), 9–19.
17. Cappelletti, M, Garth, B. (1978). Access to Justice: The Newest Wave in the Worldwide Movement to Make Rights Effective. *Buffalo Law Review, 27*(2),181–292.
18. Beqiraj, J., McNamara, L. (2014). *International Access to Justice: Barriers and Solutions, Bingham Centre for the Rule of Law Report.* International Bar

Association. Available from: https://www.cfcj-fcjc.org/sites/default/files/344/international-access-to-justice.pdf

19. Bondy, V., Mulcahy, L. Doyle, M., Reid, V. (2009). *Mediation and Judicial Review: An Empirical Research Study.* The Public Law Project.
20. Alexander, N., Giorgadze, V., Goh, A. (2020). *SIDRA International Dispute Resolution Survey: Final Report.* Singapore International Dispute Resolution Academy. Available from: https://sidra.smu.edu.sg/sites/sidra.smu.edu.sg/files/survey/index.html
21. Alexander, N., Abala, ART., Feng, SLH., Lopez, S., Ern, JPS., En, RTX. (2022). *SIDRA International Dispute Resolution Survey: 2022 Final Report.* Singapore International Dispute Resolution Academy. Available from: https://sidra.smu.edu.sg/sites/sidra.smu.edu.sg/files/survey-2022/index.html?1
22. De Palo, G., Feasley, A., Orecchini, F. (2011). *Quantifying the Cost of Not Using Mediation — A Data Analysis.* Directorate-General for Internal Policies, European Parliament.
23. Lawrence, A., Nugent, J., Scarfone, C. (2007). *The Effectiveness of Using Mediation in Selected Civil Law Disputes: A Meta-Analysis.* Department of Justice, Canada. Available from: https://publications.gc.ca/collections/collection_2009/justice/J3-2-2007-3E.pdf
24. Giacalone, M., Salehi, SS. (2022). An Empirical Study on Mediation in Civil and Commercial Disputes in Europe: The Mediation Service Providers Perspective. *Revista ítalo-española de Derecho Procesal, 2*, 11–54.
25. Bondy, V., Mulcahy, L., Doyle, M., Reid, V. (2009). *Mediation and Judicial Review: An Empirical Research Study.* The Public Law Project.
26. Quek, D. (2020). Mandatory Mediation: An Oxymoron — Examining the Feasibility of Implementing a Court-Mandated Mediation Program. *Cardozo Journal of Conflict Resolution, 11,* 479–510.
27. De Palo, G., Feasley, A., Orecchini, F. (2011). *Quantifying the Cost of Not Using Mediation — A Data Analysis.* Directorate-General for Internal Policies, European Parliament.
28. Bondy, V., Mulcahy, L., Doyle, M., Reid, V. (2009). *Mediation and Judicial Review: An Empirical Research Study.* The Public Law Project.
29. Seth, R. (2000). *Mediation: The Great Equalizer? A Critical Theory Analysis.* Canadian Forum for Civil Justice. Available from: https://www.cfcj-fcjc.org/sites/default/files/docs/hosted/16171-mediation_equalizer.pdf
30. Shapira, O. (2009). Exploring the Concept of Power in Mediation: Mediators' Sources of Power and Influence Tactics. *Ohio State Journal on Dispute Resolution, 24*, 535–569.

31. Gewurz, IG. (2001). (Re)Designing Mediation to Address the Nuances of Power Imbalance. *Conflict Resolution Quarterly, 19*(2), 135–162.
32. Ibid.
33. Greenberg, MS., Blazina, MA. (2004). What Mediators Need to Know about Class Actions: A Basic Primer. *Hamline Law Review, 27*, 191–224.
34. Claxton, J. (2021). Mediators Like Online Mediation And Other Verifiable Facts. Mediate.com. Available from: https://mediate.com/mediators-like-online-mediation-and-other-verifiable-facts/
35. Poole, A. (2014). *Baraza Justice: A Case Study of Community Led Conflict Resolution in D. R. Congo.* Peace Direct. Available from: https://www.peacedirect.org/wp-content/uploads/2023/09/Baraza-Justice-full.pdf
36. ADR Institute of Canada. (2021). *Trauma Informed Dispute Resolution — A Practical Process*. ADR Institute of Canada. Available from: https://adric.ca/trauma-informed-dispute-resolution-a-practical-process/
37. Lanni, A. (2022). Community-based and Restorative Justice Interventions To Reduce Over-Policing. *American Journal of Law and Equity, 2*, 69–84.

Chapter 4 Mediating with the Mahabharata: Investigating the Parties' Influence on Success and Failure in Mediation

1. JAMS. Mediation defined [Internet]. [cited 2025 Aug 1]. Available from: https://www.jamsadr.com/mediation-defined/
2. Vyas, (2020) Vol. 3, Udyogparv, Chapter 127, Verse 25
3. Bhaktivedanta Swami Prabhupada A.C. (2008) *The Bhagavad-Gita As It Is*. The Bhaktivedanta Book Trust. (Original work published ca. 2nd century B.C.E)

Chapter 5 Unravelling Neutrality: Examining Neutrality as a Core Mediation Principle in Facilitative and Evaluative Mediation Models

1. Alexander, N. (2012). Towards a greater global understanding of what mediators do. *Kluwer Mediation Blog* [Internet]. Available from: https://mediationblog.kluwerarbitration.com/2012/10/06/towards-a-greater-global-understanding-of-what-mediators-do/

2. Kishore, S. (2006). The Evolving Concepts of Neutrality and Impartiality in Mediation. *Commonwealth Law Bulletin, 32*(2), 221–5.
3. National Alternative Dispute Resolution Advisory Council. (2015). National Mediator Accreditation System. 11. Available from: https://msb.org.au/themes/msb/assets/documents/national-mediator-accreditation-system.pdf
4. Astor, H. (2007). Mediator neutrality: Making sense of theory and practice. *Social & Legal Studies. 16*(2), 221–39.
5. Riskin, L. (1994). Mediator Orientations, Strategies and Techniques. *Alternative to the High Cost Litigation, 12*(9):111–2.
6. Pincen, T. (1994). Joseph Elder: Quiet Peacemaking in a Civil War. *When Talk Works,* 513.
7. Choo, S. (2007). From Innocence to Experience: Lessons from Interviews with Four Experienced Mediators in Singapore. *Asian Journal of Mediation, 6.*
8. Harvard Law School. What is a Neutral Third Party? Program on Negotiation [Internet]. [cited 2025 Aug 1]. Available from: https://www.pon.harvard.edu/tag/neutral-third-party/
9. Astor. H. (2007). Mediator neutrality: Making sense of theory and practice. *Social & Legal Studies, 16(*2), 221–39.
10. *Cross Border Mediation: Professional Skills and Practice, Participant Handbook.* (2021). Chapter 9, 7.2.
11. Singapore International Mediation Institute. Annex A, Ethics of Mediation, Competency Framework for Mediators. (2023). Available from: https://www.simi.org.sg/What-We-Offer/Mediators/The-SIMI-Competency-Framework-for-Mediators
12. Coben, J. (2004). Gollum, Meet Smeagol: A Schizophrenic Rumination on Mediator Values Beyond Self Determination and Neutrality. *Cardozo Journal of Conflict Resolution, 5,* 65–91.
13. Ibid.
14. Chua, E. (2013). Moving beyond the Facilitative and Evaluative Divide: Considering Techniques that can Further the Goals of Mediation. *Asian Journal on Mediation, 37*, 37–49.
15. Kovach, KK., Love, LP. (1996). 'Evaluative Mediation' is an Oxymoron. *Alternatives to the High Cost Litigation, 14(*3). 31–2.
16. Quek, D. (2013). Facilitative Versus Evaluative Mediation: Is there Necessarily a Dichotomy? *Asian Journal on Mediation, 66.*
17. Alexander, N. (2018). Hong Kong: Mediation and the Future of Dispute Resolution. *Conflict Resolution in Asia: Mediation and other Cultural Models,* 183–218.

18. International Mediation Institute. Olé! Concise Case Analysis & Evaluation Tool [Internet]. [cited 2025 Aug 1]. Available from: https://imimediation.org/wp-content/uploads/2017/09/Ol%c3%a9-Case-Evaluation-Tool.pdf
19. Singapore International Mediation Institute. Annex A, Ethics of Mediation, Competency Framework for Mediators. (2023). Available from: https://www.simi.org.sg/What-We-Offer/Mediators/The-SIMI-Competency-Framework-for-Mediators
20. Jones, W., Hughes, S. (2003). Complexity, Conflict Resolution, and How the Mind Works. *Conflict Resolution Quarterly, 20*(4), 485–94.
21. *Cross Border Mediation: Professional Skills and Practice, Participant Handbook.* (2021). Chapter 9, 7.2.
22. Mayer, B. (2004). *Beyond Neutrality: Confronting the Crisis in Conflict Resolution.* 1st ed. San Francisco: Jossey-Bass.
23. Singapore International Dispute Resolution Academy. (2022). *Survey Final Report,* 6.4.
24. Chatterjee, P., Singhania, A., Goel, B. (2023). Third-Party Funding: Treading on Thin Ice? *Kluwer Arbitration Blog* [Internet [cited 2025 Aug 1]. Available from: https://arbitrationblog.kluwerarbitration.com/2023/08/27/third-party-funding-treading-on-thin-ice/
25. Mayer, B. (2004). *Beyond Neutrality: Confronting the Crisis in Conflict Resolution.* 1st ed. San Francisco: Jossey-Bass.
26. History.com Editors. Camp David Accords [Internet]. 2019 Nov 14 [cited 2025 Aug 1]. Available from: https://www.history.com/topics/middle-east/camp-david-accords
27. Goodreads. Desmond Tutu Quotes [Internet]. [cited 2025 Aug 1]. Available from: https://www.goodreads.com/quotes/7424-if-you-are-neutral-in-situations-of-injustice-you-have
28. Lee, J., Teh, HH. (2009). An Asian Perspective on Mediation. *Singapore: Academy Publishing,* 4.9.
29. Sharp, G. (2012) Biased is better and impartiality is in. *Kluwer Mediation Blog* [Internet]. [cited 2025 Aug 1]. Available from: https://mediationblog.kluwerarbitration.com/2012/10/01/biased-is-better-and-impartiality-is-in/
30. Goldberg, SB. (2005). The Secrets of Successful Mediators. *Negotiation Journal*, 365–76.
31. Gross, EK. (1999). Evaluating/Assessment of Navajo Peacemaking. National Institute of Justice. Available from: https://www.ojp.gov/pdffiles1/nij/grants/187675.pdf

32. Mayer, B. (2004). *Beyond Neutrality: Confronting the Crisis in Conflict Resolution.* 1st ed. San Francisco: Jossey-Bass.
33. Rajah, M. (2015). Cooking Curry in a Cultural Melting Pot: An Argument for a Mandatory "Community Mediation" framework in Singapore. *Asian Journal on Mediation.*
34. Mayer, B. (2004). *Beyond Neutrality: Confronting the Crisis in Conflict Resolution.* 1st ed. San Francisco: Jossey-Bass.
35. Australian Mediation Association. National Mediator Accreditation System [Internet]. [cited 2025 Aug 1]. Available from: https://ama.asn.au/mediator-accreditation/#Approval-%20Standards
36. Alexander, N. (2017). Cultural Confusion — a good thing for mediation? *Kluwer Mediation Blog* [Internet]. [cited 2025 Aug 1]. Available from: https://ink.library.smu.edu.sg/sol_research/3313/
37. Pincen, T. (1994). Joseph Elder: Quiet Peacemaking in a Civil War. *When Talk Works,* 513.
38. Choo, S. (2007). From Innocence to Experience: Lessons from Interviews with Four Experienced Mediators in Singapore. *Asian Journal of Mediation, 6.*
39. Lande, J. (1997). How Will Lawyering and Mediation Practices Transform Each Other? *Florida State University Law Review, 24*(4), 839–902.
40. Stulberg, JB. (1997). Facilitative versus Evaluative Mediator Orientations: Piercing the 'Grid' Lock. *Florida State University Law Review, 24,* 985–1006.
41. Miller, A. (2023) Facilitative and Evaluative Models of Mediation: Is the Distinction Still Meaningful, or Simply Arcane Semantics? Is it Time to Bring Evaluative Mediation out of the Shadows? Singapore Convention Week.
42. Roberts, KM. (2007). Mediating the Evaluative–Facilitative Debate: Why Both Parties Are Wrong and a Proposal for Settlement. *Loyola University Chicago Law Journal, 39*(1),187–226.
43. Ury, W. The Third Side [Internet]. [cited 2025 Aug 1]. Available from: https://thirdside.williamury.com/what-is-the-third-side/
44. Cloke, K. (2001). *Mediating Dangerously, the Frontiers of Conflict Resolution.* San Francisco: Jossey-Bass.
45. Chua, E. (2013). Moving beyond the Facilitative and Evaluative Divide: Considering Techniques that can Further the Goals of Mediation. *Asian Journal on Mediation, 37*, 37–49.

Chapter 6 Two Pieces of a Puzzle: A Collaborative Reading of the Singapore Convention and the New York Convention

1. Ray, A. (2019). Is Singapore Convention to Mediation what New York Convention is to Arbitration? *Kluwer Arbitration Blog* [Internet]. [cited 2025 Aug 1]. Available from: https://arbitrationblog.kluwerarbitration.com/2019/08/31/is-singapore-convention-to-mediation-what-new-york-convention-is-to-arbitration/
2. United Nations Commission on International Trade Law. Report of Working Group II (Arbitration and Conciliation) on the work of its sixty-third session. (2015). Available from: https://documents.un.org/doc/undoc/gen/v15/065/85/pdf/v1506585.pdf
3. Ibid.
4. Ibid.
5. United Nations Convention on International Settlement Agreements Resulting from Mediation. (2018).
6. United Nations Commission on International Trade Law. Report of Working Group II (Arbitration and Conciliation) on the work of its sixty-third session. (2015). Available from: https://documents.un.org/doc/undoc/gen/v15/065/85/pdf/v1506585.pdf
7. United Nations Convention on International Settlement Agreements Resulting from Mediation. (2018).
8. Ibid.
9. United Nations Commission on International Trade Law. Report of Working Group II (Arbitration and Conciliation) on the work of its sixty-third session. (2015). Available from: https://documents.un.org/doc/undoc/gen/v15/065/85/pdf/v1506585.pdf
10. United Nations Convention on International Settlement Agreements Resulting from Mediation. (2018).
11. United Nations. Consideration of the Draft Convention on the Recognition and Enforcement of Foreign Arbitral Awards (Item 4 of the Agenda). (1958). Available from: https://documents.un.org/doc/undoc/ltd/n58/125/88/pdf/n5812588.pdf
12. Masucci, D., Ravala, MS. (2018). The Singapore Convention: A First Look. *New York Dispute Resolution Lawyer, 11*(2). Available from: https://imimediation.org/wp-content/uploads/2018/10/Singapore-Convention-Article-MSR-Pages.pdf

13. Ali, SF. (2021). *Forming Transnational Dispute Settlement Norms.* Edward Elgar Publishing Limited; p. 101.
14. Singapore Management University, Singapore International Dispute Resolution Academy. SIDRA International Dispute Resolution Survey. (2022).
15. Strong, SI. (2018). Truth in a Post-Truth Society: How Sticky Defaults, Status Quo Bias and the Sovereign Prerogative Influence the Perceived Legitimacy of International Arbitration. *University of Illinois Law Review.*
16. Singapore Management University, Singapore International Dispute Resolution Academy. SIDRA International Dispute Resolution Survey. (2022).
17. Ng, C. (2019). The Arb-Med-Arb Protocol: Promising in Concept, Problematic in Design. *Singapore Academy of Law Journal.*
18. Ibid.
19. Ibid.

Chapter 7 Safeguards or Overregulation? A Dive into Mediator Standards under the Singapore Convention

1. United Nations. United Nations Convention on International Settlement Agreements Resulting from Mediation. (2018).
2. 793 So2d 1095 (Fla Dist Ct App 2001).
3. Tan, Y. (2022). An Analysis of Mediators' Misconducts Relating to Articles 5(1)(E) and 5(1)(F) of the Singapore Convention on Mediation. *Bristol Law Review,* 115–42.
4. Gardner, NT. (1986). Mediation: A Comprehensive Guide to Resolving Conflicts Without Litigation. *Michigan Law Review, 84*:1036–41.
5. United Nations. United Nations Convention on the Recognition and Enforcement of Foreign Arbitral Awards. (1958).
6. Tan, Y. (2022). An Analysis of Mediators' Misconducts Relating to Articles 5(1)(E) and 5(1)(F) of the Singapore Convention on Mediation. (2022). *Bristol Law Review*, 115–42.
7. Anderson, Q., Choo, K. (2012). Mediation advocacy for civil disputes in the Subordinate Courts: Perspectives from the bench. *Singapore Law Gazette.*
8. UNCITRAL. Report of Working Group II (Dispute Settlement) on the work of its sixty-seventh session. (2017).
9. Tetunic, FL. (2017) The Irony of Mediator as Problem Maker: Mediator Misconduct Setting Aside Mediated Agreements. *Harvard Negotiation Law Review, 23*:177–8.

10. Goncalves, A., Bogacz, F., Rainey, D. (2019). Beyond the Singapore Convention: the Importance of Creating A 'Code of Disclosure' to Make International Commercial Mediation Mainstream. *International Journal of Online Dispute Resolution, 6*(2):164–9.
11. Ibid.
12. Hofstede, G. (1984). Culture's Consequences: International Differences in Work-Related Values. 2nd ed. Beverly Hills CA: SAGE Publications.
13. Goncalves, A., Bogacz, F., Rainey, D. (2019). Beyond the Singapore Convention: the Importance of Creating A 'Code of Disclosure' to Make International Commercial Mediation Mainstream. *International Journal of Online Dispute Resolution*, 6(2):164–9.

Chapter 8 Should Third-Party Funding Be Extended to Stand-alone Mediation?

1. Ministry of Law Singapore. (2021, June 21). *Third-party Funding to be Permitted for More Categories of Legal Proceedings in Singapore*. Retrieved from: https://www.mlaw.gov.sg/news/press-releases/2021-06-21-third-party-funding-framework-permitted-for-more-categories-of-legal-preceedings-in-singapore/.
2. Columbia Centre on Sustainable Investment. (n.d.) *Concern: Third Party Funding*. Retrieved from: https://ccsi.columbia.edu/sites/default/files/content/docs/short%20note%20-%20third%20party%20funding.pdf
3. Ministry of Law Singapore. *Second Reading Speech by Senior Minister of State for Law, Indranee Rajah SC, on the Civil Law (Amendment) Bill 2016* [Internet]. 2017 Jan 10 [cited 2025 Oct 16]. Retrieved from: https://www.mlaw.gov.sg/news/parliamentary-speeches/second-reading-speech-by-senior-minister-of-state-for-law--indra3/
4. Chatterjee, P., Singhania, A., Goel, B. (2023). *Third-party funding: treading on thin ice?* Kluwer Arbitration Blog [Internet]. 2023 Aug 27 [cited 2025 Oct 16]. Available from: https://arbitrationblog.kluwerarbitration.com/2023/08/27/third-party-funding-treading-on-thin-ice/
5. Ministry of Law Singapore. (2017, January 10). Second Reading Speech by Senior Minister of State for Law, Indranee Rajah SC, on the Civil Law (Amendment) Bill 2016. Retrieved from: https://www.mlaw.gov.sg/news/parliamentary-speeches/second-reading-speech-by-senior-minister-of-state-for-law--indra3/
6. Ministry of Law (Singapore). (2021). *Third-Party Funding to be Permitted for More Categories of Legal Proceedings in Singapore* [Press release on the

Internet]. 2021 Jun 21 [cited 2025 Oct 16]. Available from: https://www.mlaw.gov.sg/news/press-releases/2021-06-21-third-party-funding-framework-permitted-for-more-categories-of-legal-preceedings-in-singapore/

7. PwC. *Redefining dispute resolution.* [Thought leadership report]. PwC Singapore.
8. Rajah, I. (2017). *Second Reading Speech on the Civil Law (Amendment) Bill 2016.* Singapore Parliament Hansard. 2017 Jan 10.
9. Arbitration Act (2001) (Singapore). (Cap. 10, 2002 Rev. Ed.).
10. Thevar, N. *Third-party funding and the pitfalls of privilege.* Practical Law Arbitration Blog [Internet]. Available from: http://arbitrationblog.practicallaw.com/third-party-funding-and-the-pitfalls-of-privilege/.
11. Singapore International Arbitration Centre. (2016). *SIAC Arbitration Rules.* 6th ed. Singapore: SIAC.
12. Greenberg, EE. (2021). *Please ask, please tell: Disclosing third-party funding in mediation.* St. John's Legal Studies Research Paper No. 21-0015. Available from: https://ssrn.com/abstract=3864248.
13. Taylor, K. (2015, April 6). *Mediation: Confidentiality and Enforceability of the Process.* Retrieved from: https://www.jamsadr.com/blog/2015/mediation-confidentiality-and-enforceability.
14. Greenberg, EE. (2021). *Please ask, please tell: Disclosing third-party funding in mediation.* St. John's Legal Studies Research Paper No. 21-0015. Available from: https://ssrn.com/abstract=3864248.
15. Taylor, K. (2015, April 6). *Mediation: Confidentiality and Enforceability of the Process.* Retrieved from: https://www.jamsadr.com/blog/2015/mediation-confidentiality-and-enforceability.
16. Greenberg, E. (2021). *Please Ask, Please Tell: Disclosing Third-Party Funding in Mediation.* Arizona State Law Journal, Volume 51 (Issue 1), 145.
17. Salem, R. (2003, July). *Trust in Mediation.* Retrieved from: https://www.beyondintractability.org/essay/trust_mediation
18. McGovern, F. E. (2016). *Trust and the SRBA Mediation.* 52 Idaho Law Review, 335-340.
19. Reeves, B. A. (2017, August). *How third-party funders change the chemistry of settlements.* Plaintiff. Retrieved from: https://plaintiffmagazine.com/images/issues/2017/08-august/reprints/Reeves_How-third-party-funders-change-the-chemistry-of-settlements_Plaintiff-magazine.pdf
20. Ibid.
21. Ibid.
22. Ibid.
23. Ibid.

24. Ibid.
25. Broderick, Bozimo & Company. (2023). *Third-party funding in arbitration*: Pros and cons.
26. Reeves, B. A. (2017, August). *How third-party funders change the chemistry of settlements*. Plaintiff. Retrieved from: https://plaintiffmagazine.com/images/issues/2017/08-august/reprints/Reeves_How-third-party-funders-change-the-chemistry-of-settlements_Plaintiff-magazine.pdf
27. Ibid.
28. Ibid.
29. Columbia Center on Sustainable Investment. Concern: *Third-Party Funding.* [Issue brief]. Retrieved from: https://ccsi.columbia.edu/sites/default/files/content/docs/short%20note%20-%20third%20party%20funding.pdf
30. Ashurst. *Third Party Funding in International Arbitration*. 2022 Jun 15. Retrieved from: https://www.ashurst.com/en/insights/quickguide-third-party-funding-in-international-arbitration/
31. Aceris Law. (2024, April 23). *The Drawbacks of Third-Party Funding For Arbitration*. Retrieved from https://www.mondaq.com/arbitration--dispute-resolution/1453382/the-drawbacks-of-third-party-funding-for-arbitration
32. Broderick Bozimo & Company. *Third-Party Funding in Arbitration: Pros and Cons*. 2024 Apr 23. Retrieved from: Third-Party Funding in Arbitration: Pros and Cons (broderickbozimo.com)
33. Reeves, BA. *How third-party funders change the chemistry of settlements. Advocate — Journal of Consumer Attorneys Associations for Southern California.* 2017 Sep.
34. Law Society of Singapore. *Guidance Note 10.1.1 — Third-Party Funding*. 2017 Apr 25. Available from: https://www.mlaw.gov.sg/files/Council_GN_Third_Party_Funding.pdf
35. Macnab, A. (2024). *Collaborative, interest-based dispute resolution trending in international commercial arbitration. Canadian Lawyer.*
36. Smyth, D., Maguiness, M. (2019). Third-Party Funding of Arbitration (and Mediation) in Hong Kong. *Hong Kong Lawyer.* 2024 Jan 25. Available from: https://www.canadianlawyermag.com/practice-areas/adr/collaborative-interest-based-dispute-resolution-trending-in-international-commercial-arbitration/383150
37. Sahani, V. S. (2015, February). *Harmonizing Third-Party Litigation Funding Regulation*. Cardozo Law Review. Retrieved from: https://papers.ssrn.com/sol3/papers.cfm?abstract_id=2419686#
38. Ibid.
39. Papadas, A. (2020). *Third-Party Funding and Mediation*. Lexology (Augusta Ventures).

40. Sahani, V. S. (2017, February). *Reshaping Third-Party Funding*. Tulane Law Review, Volume 91, 448. Retrieved from: https://scholarlycommons.law.wlu.edu/cgi/viewcontent.cgi?article=1513&context=wlufac
41. Aceris Law. (2024, April 23). *The Drawbacks of Third-Party Funding For Arbitration*. Retrieved from https://www.mondaq.com/arbitration--dispute-resolution/1453382/the-drawbacks-of-third-party-funding-for-arbitration
42. Columbia Center on Sustainable Investment. Concern: *Third-Party Funding*. [Issue brief]. Retrieved from: https://ccsi.columbia.edu/sites/default/files/content/docs/short%20note%20-%20third%20party%20funding.pdf
43. Aceris Law. (2024, April 23). *The Drawbacks of Third-Party Funding For Arbitration*. Retrieved from https://www.mondaq.com/arbitration--dispute-resolution/1453382/the-drawbacks-of-third-party-funding-for-arbitration
44. Ibid.
45. Ibid.
46. Norton Rose Fulbright. (2016). *The third-party funding debate — we look at the risks*. 2016 Sep. Available from: https://www.nortonrosefulbright.com/en/knowledge/publications/6c843d32/the-third-party-funding-debate---we-look-at-the-risks
47. Broderick, Bozimo & Company. (2023). Th*ird-party funding in arbitration: Pros and cons*. 2023 Oct 24. Available from: https://broderickbozimo.com/third-party-funding-in-arbitration-pros-and-cons/
48. Norton Rose Fulbright. (2016). *The third-party funding debate — we look at the risks*. 2016 Sep. Available from: https://www.nortonrosefulbright.com/en/knowledge/publications/6c843d32/the-third-party-funding-debate---we-look-at-the-risks
49. Aceris Law. (2024, April 23). *The Drawbacks of Third-Party Funding For Arbitration*. Retrieved from https://www.mondaq.com/arbitration--dispute-resolution/1453382/the-drawbacks-of-third-party-funding-for-arbitration
50. Omni Bridgeway. (2022). *The current approach to recovering third party funding costs in arbitration*. 2022 Jan 12. Retrieved from https://omnibridgeway.com/insights/blog/blog-posts/blog-details/global/2022/01/12/the-current-approach-to-recovering-third-party-funding-costs-in-arbitration
51. International Council for Commercial Arbitration. (2018, April). *Report of the ICCA-Queen Mary Task Force on Third-Party Funding in International Arbitration*, 23-24.
52. Smyth, D., Maguiness, M. (2019). Third-Party Funding of Arbitration (and Mediation) in Hong Kong. *Hong Kong Lawyer.* 2024 Jan 25. Available from: https://www.canadianlawyermag.com/practice-areas/adr/collaborative-interest-based-dispute-resolution-trending-in-international-commercial-arbitration/383150.

53. Columbia Center on Sustainable Investment. Concern: *Third-Party Funding.* [Issue brief]. Retrieved from: https://ccsi.columbia.edu/sites/default/files/content/docs/short%20note%20-%20third%20party%20funding.pdf
54. Ibid.
55. Smyth, D., Maguiness, M. (2019). Third-Party Funding of Arbitration (and Mediation) in Hong Kong. *Hong Kong Lawyer.* 2024 Jan 25. Available from: https://www.canadianlawyermag.com/practice-areas/adr/collaborative-interest-based-dispute-resolution-trending-in-international-commercial-arbitration/383150
56. Ibid.

Chapter 9 Cultural Dynamics in International Mediation: Anthropological Insights for Effective Conflict Resolution

1. Encyclopedia Britannica. (1998). Mediation: Conflict Resolution, Diplomacy & Negotiation.
2. Lucke, K., Rigaut, A. (2002). Cultural issues in international mediation. EU as Mediator.
3. Nicolas, A. (2020). What Is Mediation?: Definitions and Anthropological Discomforts. In: Härter, K., Hillemanns, C., Schlee, G., editors. *On Mediation: Historical, Legal, Anthropological and International Perspectives.* 1st ed. Vol. 22. Berghahn Books; p. 69–94.
4. Menkel-Meadow, C., Abramson, HI. (2011). Mediating multiculturally: Culture and the ethical mediator. In: Waldman, E., editor. *Mediation ethics: Cases & commentaries*. Jossey-Bass. p. 305–38.
5. Gellman, M. (2007). Powerful cultures: Indigenous and Western conflict resolution processes in Cambodian peacebuilding. *Journal of Peace, Conflict and Development, (11).*
6. Leslie, CM., Varenne, H., Jeganathan, P., Spencer, JR., Kolata, AL, Paul, RA, *et al.* (2024). Anthropology. In*: Encyclopedia Britannica.*
7. Encyclopedia Britannica. (2016). Cultural imperialism.
8. Lampe, JR. (2009). Bosnian War. *Encyclopedia Britannica.*
9. Office of the High Representative. Annex 4: Constitution of Bosnia and Herzegovina.
10. Borger, J. (2015). Bosnia's bitter, flawed peace deal, 20 years on. *The Guardian.*
11. Vrasti, W. (2008). The strange case of ethnography and international relations. *Millennium: Journal of International Studies, 37*(2):279–301.

12. ScienceDirect Topics. Cultural relativism.
13. Human Rights Watch. (2022). Myanmar: No Justice, No Freedom for Rohingya 5 Years On.
14. Howell, S. (2023). Ethnography. *Open Encyclopedia of Anthropology.*
15. Seligman, R., Brown, RA. (2010). Theory and method at the intersection of anthropology and cultural neuroscience. *Social Cognitive and Affective Neuroscience, 5*(2–3):130–7.
16. Lees, S., Havini, M., Murdock, J., Vienings, T. Bougainville Peace Agreement: The Burnham I and II Dialogues. Namgyal, J., editor. United Nations Development Programme.
17. Bass, GJ. (2004). Jus post bellum. *Philosophy & Public Affairs, 32*(4).
18. United States Institute of Peace. (2021). Healing the Wounds of War with the Vietnam Wartime Accounting Initiative.
19. Sellström, T., Wohlgemuth, L. (1996). The international response to conflict and genocide: Lessons from the Rwanda experience: Study 1: Historical perspective: Some explanatory factors. The Nordic Africa Institute.
20. BBC News. (2019). Rwanda genocide: 100 days of slaughter.
21. United Nations Security Council. (1994). Resolution 912.
22. Hauschildt, T. (2012). Gacaca courts and restorative justice in Rwanda. E-International Relations.
23. Gottlieb, A., Hart, RD. (2023). At the heart of the Israel-Palestinian conflict, anthropology matters as much as history. *The Hill.*
24. Hammad, F. (2023). A brief history of the US-Israel ‘special relationship’ shows how connections have shifted since long before the 1948 founding of the Jewish state. *USC Dornsife News.*
25. Beaumont, P. (2020). Trump’s Middle East peace plan: key points at a glance. *The Guardian.*
26. Young, M. (2023). Israel’s landscapes of subjugation. Carnegie Endowment for International Peace.
27. Imperial War Museums. What You Need to Know About The Troubles.
28. Lawless, J. (2023). As it turns 25, N Ireland’s Good Friday Agreement explained. *AP News.*
29. Spencer, G. (2005). The Northern Ireland Peace Process. In: *The Media and Peace*. London: Palgrave Macmillan.
30. Scham, P., Pogrund, B., Ghanem, A. (2013). Introduction to Shared Narratives — A Palestinian-Israeli Dialogue. *Israel Studies, 18*(2):1–10.
31. Wheeler, R. (2017). Ruth Benedict and the Purpose of Anthropology. The Peabody.

Chapter 10 Charting Twin Pursuits — Reconciling the Tension Between Confidentiality as a Procedural Feature and the State's Interest in Pursuing Transparency in Mediating Investor-State Disputes

1. Morek, R. (2013). Nihil silentio utilius: Confidentiality in mediation and its legal safeguards in the EU Member States. *ERA Forum, 14*:421–35.
2. de la Rasilla, I. (2023). "The Greatest Victory": Challenges and Opportunities for Mediation in Investor-State Dispute Settlement. *ICSID Review, 38*(1):169–200.
3. Coe, JJ Jr. (2005). Toward a Complementary Use of Conciliation in Investor-State Disputes — A Preliminary Search. *UC Davis Journal of International Law & Policy, 12*(7).
4. Quek Anderson, D. (2019). Piercing the veil of confidentiality in mediation to ensure good faith participation — An untenable position? *Singapore Academy of Law Journal, 31*:709–41.
5. Morek, R. (2013). Nihil silentio utilius: Confidentiality in mediation and its legal safeguards in the EU Member States. *ERA Forum,14*:421–35.
6. Fan, X. (2022). The Confidentiality and Transparency Debate Under Investor-State Mediation. *Groningen Journal of International Law, 9*(2):325–51.
7. Mediation of Investor-State Conflicts. (2014). *Harvard Law Review, 127*(8):2543–64.
8. National University of Singapore, Centre for International Law. Getting the Most Out of the Singapore Convention in Investor-State Disputes.
9. Fan, X. (2022). The Confidentiality and Transparency Debate Under Investor-State Mediation. *Groningen Journal of International Law, 9*(2):325–51.
10. Magraw, D., Plagakis, S., Schifano, J. (2008). Ways and Means of Citizens' Participation in Trade and Investment Dispute Settlement Procedures. *SSRN Electronic Journal.*
11. Sharma, R. (2020). Mediation of Investor-State Disputes: Should It Be Transparent? *Contemporary Asia Arbitration Journal,13*(2).
12. United Nations Conference on Trade and Development. (2010). Investor-state disputes: Prevention and alternatives to arbitration. United Nations.
13. United Nations Commission on International Trade Law. (2017). *Report of Working Group III (Investor-State Dispute Settlement Reform) on the Work of Its Thirty-Fourth Session — Part I (UN Doc A/CN.9/930/Rev 1).*

14. Ali, SF., Repousis, OG. (2017). Investor-State Mediation and the Rise of Transparency in International Investment Law: Opportunity or Threat. *Denver Journal of International Law & Policy, 45*:225–52.
15. Alexander, N., Steffek, F. (2016). Making Mediation Law.
16. Morek, R. (2013). Nihil silentio utilius: Confidentiality in mediation and its legal safeguards in the EU Member States. *ERA Forum,14*:421–35.
17. Fan, X. (2022). The Confidentiality and Transparency Debate Under Investor-State Mediation. *Groningen Journal of International Law, 9*(2):325–51.
18. Sharma, R. (2020). Mediation of Investor-State Disputes: Should It Be Transparent? *Contemporary Asia Arbitration Journal,13*(2).
19. International Centre for Settlement of Investment Disputes. (2022). ICSID Mediation Rules [Internet]. Available from: https://icsid.worldbank.org/sites/default/files/documents/ICSID_Mediation.pdf
20. Brown, C., Winch, P. (2019). The Confidentiality and Transparency Debate in Commercial and Investment. In: Titi C, Gómez KF, editors. *Mediation in International Commercial and Investment Disputes*. Oxford University Press.
21. Fan, K. (2020). Mediation of Investor–State Disputes: A Treaty Survey. *Journal of Dispute Resolution, 2.*
22. Freedman, LR., Prigoff, ML. (1986). Confidentiality in mediation: The need for protection. *Ohio State Journal on Dispute Resolution, 2*(1).
23. Singapore International Dispute Resolution Academy. *SIDRA International Dispute Resolution Survey: 2020 Final Report.*
24. Chew, S., Lucy, R., Thomas, CJ. (2018). Report: Survey on Obstacles to Settlement of Investor-State Disputes. *SSRN Electronic Journal.*
25. Titi, C., Gómez, KF. (2019). Mediation in International Commercial and Investment Disputes. *Oxford University Press.*
26. Kessedjian, C., van Aaken, A., Lie, R., Mistelis, L., Reis, JM. (2023). Mediation in Future Investor–State Dispute Settlement. *Journal of International Dispute Settlement,14(*2):192–212.
27. Ali, SF., Repousis, OG. (2017). Investor-State Mediation and the Rise of Transparency in International Investment Law: Opportunity or Threat. *Denver Journal of International Law & Policy, 45*:225–52.
28. Ibid.
29. National University of Singapore, Centre for International Law. Getting the Most Out of the Singapore Convention in Investor-State Disputes.
30. Kessedjian, C., van Aaken, A., Lie, R., Mistelis, L., Reis, JM. (2023). Mediation in Future Investor–State Dispute Settlement. *Journal of International Dispute Settlement,14(*2):192–212.
31. Legum, B. (2019). The Multiple-Ministry Paradigm in Investor-State Dispute Settlement. *BCDR International Arbitration Review, 6*(2):433–40.

32. Chew, S., Lucy, R., Thomas, CJ. (2018). Report: Survey on Obstacles to Settlement of Investor-State Disputes. *SSRN Electronic Journal.*
33. Ibid.
34. Fan, X. (2022). The Confidentiality and Transparency Debate Under Investor-State Mediation. *Groningen Journal of International Law, 9*(2):325–51.
35. Singapore International Dispute Resolution Academy. *SIDRA International Dispute Resolution Survey: 2020 Final Report.*
36. International Centre for Settlement of Investment Disputes. (2018). *Proposals for Amendment of the ICSID Rules — Working Paper 1.* United Nations.
37. United Nations Commission on International Trade Law. (2015). *Report of Working Group II (Arbitration and Conciliation) on the work of its sixty-third session (A/CN.9/861).* United Nations.
38. Titi, C. (2019). Mediation and the Settlement of International Investment Disputes: Between Utopia and Realism. In: Titi, C., Gómez, KF., editors. *Mediation in International Commercial and Investment Disputes.* Oxford University Press.
39. Fan, K. (2020). Mediation of Investor–State Disputes: A Treaty Survey. *Journal of Dispute Resolution,2.*
40. Coe, JJ Jr. (2005). Toward a Complementary Use of Conciliation in Investor-State Disputes — A Preliminary Search. *UC Davis Journal of International Law & Policy,12*(7).
41. Fan, X. (2022). The Confidentiality and Transparency Debate Under Investor-State Mediation. *Groningen Journal of International Law, 9*(2):325–51.
42. Ali, SF., Repousis, OG. (2017). Investor-State Mediation and the Rise of Transparency in International Investment Law: Opportunity or Threat. *Denver Journal of International Law & Policy, 45*:225–52.
43. Alexander, N., Chong, S. (2021). The Singapore Convention on Mediation: Origins and Application to Investor–State Disputes. In: Mohan, M., Brown, C., editors. *The Asian Turn in Foreign Investment.* 1st ed. Cambridge University Press. p. 340–60.
44. Shirlow, E. (2020). Investor-State Arbitration Meets Mediation: Potential Problems? *Kluwer Arbitration Blog.*
45. ICSID Mediation Rules, Article 10(1); IBA Rules, Articles 10(1), (2).
46. ICSID Mediation Rules, Article 10(2); SCC Mediation Rules, Article 3.
47. Ibid.
48. International Energy Charter. (2016). Guide on Investment Mediation [Internet]. Guideline 10.C. Available from: https://www.energycharter.org/fileadmin/DocumentsMedia/CCDECS/2016/CCDEC201612.pdf
49. Guiguo, W. (2011). Chinese Mechanisms for Resolving Investor-State Disputes. *Jindal Journal of International Affairs, 1*(1):204–33.

50. McLaughlin, M. (2021). Investor–State Mediation and the Belt and Road Initiative: Examining the Conditions for Settlement. *Journal of International Economic Law, 24*(3):609–29.
51. People's Republic of China Ministry of Commerce. (2020). MOFCOM Order No. 3 of 2020 on Rules on Handling Complaints of Foreign-Invested Enterprises.
52. Ministry of Commerce of the People's Republic of China. Measures for the Administration of Complaints by Foreign-Invested Enterprises: Article 23 [Internet]. 2020 [cited 2024 May 10]. Available from: https://english.mofcom.gov.cn/Policies/AnnouncementsOrders/art/2020/art_f51a8baf43b54dc2af247c62d447224d.html
53. Zeinemann, R. (2024). The Characterization of Public Sector Mediation. *Environs: Envtl. L. & Pol'y J. 24.*
54. United Nations Commission on International Trade Law. (2023). *Possible reform of investor-State dispute settlement (ISDS): Annotations to the draft pro*visions on procedural and cross-cutting issues (A/CN.9/WG.III/WP.232). United Nations.
55. Reitman, JW. (2003). The Allagash: A Case Study of a Successful Environmental Mediation. *Mediate.Com.*
56. McGovern, F. (2006). Mediation of the Snake River Basin Adjudication. *Idaho L. Rev, 42*:548–53.
57. Ibid.
58. Shang, S. (2019). Implementing Investor–state Mediation in China's Next Generation Investment Treaties. In: Chaisse, J., editor. *China's International Investment Strategy.* 1st ed. Oxford University Press. p. 504–17.
59. Schneider, AK., Welsh, NA. (2021). Bargaining in the Shadow of Investor-state Mediation: How the Threat of Mediation Will Improve Parties' Conflict Management. *University of St. Thomas Law Journal, 17*:373.
60. Shirlow, E. (2020). Investor-State Arbitration Meets Mediation: Potential Problems? *Kluwer Arbitration Blog.*
61. United Nations Commission on International Trade Law. (2018). *Report of Working Group III (Investor-State Dispute Settlement Reform) on the Work of Its Thirty-Fifth Session (UN Doc A/CN.9/935).* United Nations.
62. United Nations Commission on International Trade Law. (2017). *Report of Working Group III (Investor-State Dispute Settlement Reform) on the Work of Its Thirty-Fourth Session — Part I (UN Doc A/CN.9/930/Rev 1).* United Nations.
63. United Nations Commission on International Trade Law. (2023). *Possible reform of investor-State dispute settlement (ISDS): Annotations to the draft*

provisions on procedural and cross-cutting issues (A/CN.9/WG.III/WP.232). United Nations.
64. Magraw, D., Plagakis, S., Schifano, J. (2008). Ways and Means of Citizens' Participation in Trade and Investment Dispute Settlement Procedures. *SSRN Electronic Journal.*
65. Investor-State Dispute Settlement Mediation Working Group. (2020). Unlocking Value Through Stakeholder Engagement: New Forms to Resolve Investor-State Disputes.
66. Kessedjian, C., van Aaken, A., Lie, R., Mistelis, L., Reis, JM. (2023). Mediation in Future Investor–State Dispute Settlement. *Journal of International Dispute Settlement,14(*2):192–212.
67. United Nations Conference on Trade and Development. (2010). Investor-state disputes: Prevention and alternatives to arbitration. United Nations.
68. Hafner-Burton, EM., Puig, S., Victor, DG. (2017). Against Secrecy: The Social Cost of International Dispute Settlement. *Yale Journal of International Law.*
69. Ubilava, A., Nottage, L. (2018). ICSID's New Mediation Rules: A Small but Positive Step Forward. Submission to ICSID on ICSID Rules and Regulations Amendment Process.
70. Quek Anderson, D. (2019). Piercing the veil of confidentiality in mediation to ensure good faith participation — An untenable position? *Singapore Academy of Law Journal, 31*:709–41.
71. Kessedjian, C., van Aaken, A., Lie, R., Mistelis, L., Reis, JM. (2023). Mediation in Future Investor–State Dispute Settlement. *Journal of International Dispute Settlement,14(*2):192–212.
72. Johnson, L., Guven, BS. (2017). The Settlement of Investment Disputes: A Discussion of Democratic Accountability and the Public Interest. *IISD Investment Treaty News.*
73. Shirlow, E. (2020). Investor-State Arbitration Meets Mediation: Potential Problems? *Kluwer Arbitration Blog.*
74. Ibid.
75. Claxton, JM. (2020). Compelling Parties to Mediate Investor-State Disputes: No Pressure, No Diamonds? *Pepperdine Dispute Resolution Law Journal.* 20:78.
76. Lai, A., Suen, M. (2020). UNCITRAL Working Group III on ISDS Reform Virtual Pre-Intersessional Meeting on the Use of Mediation in ISDS Background Paper for Session 1 — Overcoming Challenges to the Use of Mediation in ISDS. *Asian Academy of International Law.*
77. Fan, X. (2022). The Confidentiality and Transparency Debate Under Investor-State Mediation. *Groningen Journal of International Law,* 9(2):325–51.

78. United Nations Commission on International Trade Law. (2013). UNCITRAL Rules on Transparency in Treaty-based Investor-State Arbitration.
79. Magraw, D., Plagakis, S., Schifano, J. (2008). Ways and Means of Citizens' Participation in Trade and Investment Dispute Settlement Procedures. *SSRN Electronic Journal.*
80. Sharma, R. (2020). Mediation of Investor-State Disputes: Should It Be Transparent? *Contemporary Asia Arbitration Journal,13*(2).
81. Coe, JJ Jr. (2005). Toward a Complementary Use of Conciliation in Investor-State Disputes — A Preliminary Search. *UC Davis Journal of International Law & Policy,12*(7).
82. Kessedjian, C., van Aaken, A., Lie, R., Mistelis, L., Reis, JM. (2023). Mediation in Future Investor–State Dispute Settlement. *Journal of International Dispute Settlement,14(*2):192–212.
83. Fan, K. (2020). Mediation of Investor–State Disputes: A Treaty Survey. *Journal of Dispute Resolution,2.*
84. Coe, JJ Jr. (2005). Toward a Complementary Use of Conciliation in Investor-State Disputes — A Preliminary Search. *UC Davis Journal of International Law & Policy,12*(7).
85. Investor-State Dispute Settlement Mediation Working Group. (2020). Unlocking Value Through Stakeholder Engagement: New Forms to Resolve Investor-State Disputes.
86. Schneider, AK., Welsh, NA. (2021). Bargaining in the Shadow of Investor-state Mediation: How the Threat of Mediation Will Improve Parties' Conflict Management. *University of St. Thomas Law Journal, 17*:373.
87. Shang, S. (2019). Implementing Investor–state Mediation in China's Next Generation Investment Treaties. In: Chaisse, J., editor. *China's International Investment Strategy*. 1st ed. Oxford University Press. p. 504–17.
88. Ali, SF., Repousis, OG. (2017). Investor-State Mediation and the Rise of Transparency in International Investment Law: Opportunity or Threat. *Denver Journal of International Law & Policy, 45*:225–52.
89. Singapore International Dispute Resolution Academy. *SIDRA International Dispute Resolution Survey: 2020 Final Report.*
90. Schneider, AK., Welsh, NA. (2021). Bargaining in the Shadow of Investor-state Mediation: How the Threat of Mediation Will Improve Parties' Conflict Management. *University of St. Thomas Law Journal, 17*:373.
91. United Nations General Assembly. (2018). United Nations Convention on International Settlement Agreements Resulting from Mediation.
92. International Centre for Settlement of Investment Disputes. (2022). International Centre for Settlement of Investment Disputes Mediation Rules.

93. Investor-State Dispute Settlement Mediation Working Group. (2020). Unlocking Value Through Stakeholder Engagement: New Forms to Resolve Investor-State Disputes.
94. Legum, B. (2019). The Multiple-Ministry Paradigm in Investor-State Dispute Settlement. *BCDR International Arbitration Review, 6*(2):433–40.
95. International Mediation Institute. (2016). International Mediation Institute Competency Criteria for Investor-State Mediators.
96. International Energy Charter. (2016). Guide on Investment Mediation.

Chapter 11 The Risk of Settlement Regret: A Critical Factor in Counsel's Decision-Making Process?

1. Pynchon, V. (2005). Can Transformative Mediation Work in Commercial Litigation? A Conversation with Joseph P. Folger and Robert A. Baruch Bush. *Southern California Mediation Association, 14*(1):1–8.
2. Guthrie, C. (1999). Better settle than sorry: The regret aversion theory of litigation behaviour. *Univ Ill Law Rev.*, 43–90.
3. Wistrich, AJ., Rachlinski, JJ. (2013). How lawyers' intuitions prolong litigation. *South Calif Law Rev.*, *86*:571–630.
4. Guthrie, C., Korobkin, R. (1997). Psychology, economics and settlement: A new look at the role of the lawyer. *Tex Law Rev.*, *76(*1):77–141.
5. Miller, GP. (1987). Some agency problems in settlement. *J Leg Stud.*, *6*(1):189–215.
6. Lehman, DR., Lempert, RO., Nisbett, RE. (1988). The effects of graduate training on reasoning: Formal discipline and thinking about everyday-life events. *Am Psychol.*, *43*(6):431–42.
7. Wistrich, AJ., Rachlinski, JJ. (2013). How lawyers' intuitions prolong litigation. *South Calif Law Rev.*, *86*:571–630.
8. Kahneman, D., Lovallo, D. (1993). Timid choices and bold forecasts: A cognitive perspective on risk taking. *Manag Sci.*, *39(*1):17–31.
9. Tan, EKB. (2007). Harmony as ideology, culture and control: Alternative dispute resolution in Singapore. *Aust J Asian Law*, *9*(1):120–51.
10. Lim, G., Chua, E. (2017). Development of mediation in Singapore. In: McFadden D, Lim G, editors. *Mediation in Singapore: A practical guide*. 3rd ed. Singapore: Sweet and Maxwell. p. 1–24.
11. Tan, EKB. (2007). Harmony as ideology, culture and control: Alternative dispute resolution in Singapore. *Aust J Asian Law*, *9*(1):120–51.
12. Ibid.
13. State Courts Practice Directions 2021 (Singapore).

14. [2018] SGHC 208
15. [2021] NSWCA 237
16. *Chan Gek Yong v Violet Netto (practising as L F Violet Netto)* [2018] SGHC 208 at [6]
17. *Chan Gek Yong v Violet Netto (practising as L F Violet Netto)* [2018] SGHC 208 at [16]
18. *Chan Gek Yong v Violet Netto (practising as L F Violet Netto)* [2018] SGHC 208 at [67]
19. *Johnson v Firth* [2021] NSWCA 237 at [60]
20. *Johnson v Firth* [2021] NSWCA 237 at [48]
21. *Johnson v Firth* [2021] NSWCA 237 at [44]
22. *Johnson v Firth* [2021] NSWCA 237 at [75]
23. Irvine, C., Farrington, L. (2017). Mediation and emotions: Perception and regulation. In: Stannard J, Conway H, editors. *The emotional dynamics of law and legal discourse*. Oxford: Hart Publishing. p. 211–39.
24. Lind, EA. (1993). Individual and corporate dispute resolution: Using procedural fairness as a decision heuristic. *Adm Sci Q.*, *38*(2):224–51.
25. Lens, V. (2021). Therapeutic jurisprudence in family law: The role of due process. *SAL Prac.*,(21).
26. Tilbury, C. (2013). Child protection proceedings in the Children's Court in Queensland: Therapeutic opportunities lost. *Aust J Fam Law.*, *27*(2):170–87.
27. Wexler, DB. (1995). Reflections on the scope of therapeutic jurisprudence. *Psychol Public Policy Law.*, *1*(1):220–36.
28. King, MS. (2008). Restorative justice, therapeutic jurisprudence and the rise of emotionally intelligent justice. *Melb Univ Law Rev.*, *32*(3):1096–126.
29. Babb, BA. (1997). An interdisciplinary approach to family law jurisprudence: Application of an ecological and therapeutic perspective. *Indiana Law J.*, *72*(3):775–808.
30. Lens, V. (2016). Against the grain: Therapeutic judging in a traditional family court. *Law Soc Inq.*, *41*(3):701–18.
31. Nolan-Haley, JM. (2013). Judicial review of mediated settlement agreements: Improving mediation with consent. *Yearb Arbitr Mediat.*, *5*:152–61.

www.ingramcontent.com/pod-product-compliance
Lightning Source LLC
Chambersburg PA
CBHW070750281225
37357CB00004B/409
* 9 7 8 9 8 1 9 8 2 5 0 3 5 *